Praise for *The Kite and the String*

"*The Kite and the String* does not purport to be either a DIY manual or memoiristic musing. Rather, it is a guide to the stages of writing, exploring an approach which is essentially practical, human, and hopeful. . . . Mattison's close reading of various works of fiction is well worth every writer's while."

—*Los Angeles Review of Books*

"Not a how-to so much as a reflection on how to be happy, or at least productive, as a writer . . . Mattison walks us through the writing process from idea to drafting to revision, offers possible forms for stories, carefully considers issues she's noticed while teaching, then wraps up with proposals for how we might get our minds and expectations right."

—*The Rumpus*

"Full of warm but pragmatic wisdom . . . Mattison cuts through a lot of the mystique around the writing process."

—*Flavorwire*

"Alice Mattison's *The Kite and the String* is the best kind of 'inside job.' Though brimming with a practitioner's reflective wisdom and immediately useful insight, it is never prescriptive—always acknowledging that 'This worked for me . . .' without ever presuming. But Mattison is so canny and experienced that her insights are hugely relevant for all of us who write. Indeed, this book goes right next to James Wood's *How Fiction Works* on the shelf by the desk."

—Sven Birkerts, author of *The Art of Time in Memoir*

"Wry and wise, the voice of master teacher and storyteller Alice Mattison carries us aloft in this useful, funny, and important book about writing and the writing life. Every student, writer, and teacher—of fiction, nonfiction, and, for that matter, poetry—will find new insights, old truths newly expressed, and aid and comfort as we pursue our difficult and glorious art. In this book, Mattison reveals what her colleagues and students have long known—that she is an indispensable writing friend."

—April Bernard, author of *Miss Fuller*

"*The Kite and the String* is an indispensable writing guide by a master teacher, as tough-minded as it is encouraging. And Alice Mattison's wit, erudition, and transcendent common sense make it a sheer pleasure to read and reread."

—David Gates, author of *A Hand Reached Down to Guide Me*

"The essays in *The Kite and the String* are brilliant, funny, and wise—everything that readers of Alice Mattison's fine work have come to expect—and they will send you running to your desk with new insight and inspiration. Every page is a keeper."

—Jill McCorkle, author of *Life After Life*

"In this superb book about writing and her own surprising beginnings as a writer, Alice Mattison shows us how to create the vivid dream of successful fiction. If you want to be a writer, read this book."   —Susan Cheever, author of *Drinking in America*

"Mattison analyzes how to write compelling fiction in this essential guide. . . . A gold mine for writers across a spectrum of experience levels. Her conspiratorial 'we the writers' tone is charming and lively, and her breadth of knowledge makes her an effective and instructive authority. Perfect for aspiring writers or those trying to make it over a bump in the road."

—*Booklist* (starred review)

"Unlike other guides on the topic, Mattison's focuses on the process of becoming an author rather than the elements of a genre—finding story, not detailing its pieces. Anecdotes and examples from her career as a writer, mother, and MFA instructor make this a lively and provocative read. . . . The instruction is engaging and approachable, lending the feel of a writer's workshop. A great choice for writers, particularly those with a day job."

—*Library Journal* (starred review)

"A generous, empathetic writer's companion."　　—*Kirkus Reviews*

"Mattison offers thoughtful, encouraging advice. . . . She doles out guidance on crafting story, conjuring character, and keeping readers engaged, all peppered with examples taken from her own classroom as well as from the works of literary giants such as Mark Twain, George Eliot, and Tillie Olsen. Mattison pays particular attention to the difficulties women authors still face. She also opens space for discussing other types of diversity in writing, and there is plenty here that will be of enormous worth to budding novelists and memoirists of all genders, races, sexual orientations, and ages. Novice writers can do themselves (and us all) a favor by dipping into this practical primer."　　—*Publishers Weekly*

PENGUIN BOOKS

THE KITE AND THE STRING

Alice Mattison is a widely acclaimed author and longtime writing teacher. She has published six novels—including *The Book Borrower*, *Nothing Is Quite Forgotten in Brooklyn*, and *When We Argued All Night*, a *New York Times Book Review* Editors' Choice—as well as four collections of short stories and a collection of poems. Twelve of her stories have appeared in *The New Yorker*, and other work has been published in *The New York Times*, *Ploughshares*, and *Ecotone* and anthologized in *The Pushcart Prize*, *PEN/O. Henry Prize Stories*, and *Best American Short Stories*. A frequent panelist at AWP and other writing conferences, she has held residencies at Yaddo and the MacDowell Colony. She has taught at Brooklyn College, Yale University, and in the Bennington Writing Seminars, the MFA program at Bennington College.

The *Kite* and the *String*

HOW TO WRITE

WITH SPONTANEITY

AND CONTROL—

AND LIVE TO TELL THE TALE

Alice Mattison

PENGUIN BOOKS

For Sandi

PENGUIN BOOKS
An imprint of Penguin Random House LLC
375 Hudson Street
New York, New York 10014
penguin.com

First published in the United States of America by Viking Penguin,
an imprint of Penguin Random House LLC, 2016
Published in Penguin Books 2017

Portions of this book first appeared in slightly different form in the following publications:
"Tillie Olsen and the Writing of Fiction" in *The Millions* and *Bloom*; "Drowning the Children" in *The New Haven Review*; "Coincidence in Stories: An Essay Against Craft," "Silence
and Storytelling," "What Killed the Queen: And Other Uncertainties That Keep a Reader
Reading," and "Where Do You Get Your Ideas?" in *The Writer's Chronicle*.

Excerpts from "Under the dark veil my hands tensed and clutched," "Poem Without a
Hero," and other selections from *The Word That Causes Death's Defeat: Poems of Memory* by
Anna Akhmatova, translated by Nancy K. Anderson. Copyright © 2004 by Yale University.
Reprinted by permission of Yale University Press.

ISBN 9780525428541 (hardcover)
ISBN 9780143111634 (paperback)
ISBN 9780698189911 (ebook)

Printed in the United States of America
10 9 8 7 6 5 4 3 2 1

Set in Dante MT and Incognito
Designed by Nancy Resnick

Contents

Introduction: Excuse Me, Don't We Know Each Other?

Maybe you're that woman in the corner of the coffee shop. You're gazing over the lid of a laptop, then typing fast, then gazing again. Or possibly you're that man with a narrow-ruled notebook, writing fat paragraphs in black ink. Your handwriting is so dense that when you turn the page, the paper looks thick and stiff.

And I? I'm the woman with messy gray hair who's at risk of spilling her coffee down your neck, because she can't help glancing over your shoulder to get a glimpse of what you're writing. Is it, perhaps, a story? Is it a novel? A memoir? I have my own notebook or laptop, or a manuscript I'm scribbling on, but I can't seem to help sneaking a look at yours.

For decades I've been reading, writing, and teaching writing, but it seems that I haven't gotten enough of it. Oh, maybe on the last day of a writers' conference, when I've thought and talked writing for more hours than would seem possible, when I've read piles of stories, listened to hours of readings—maybe then I think, "We've got to stop this!" But a day or two later, I'm glancing over your shoulder again. And now I have written a book about writing—especially about fiction, but also of use, I hope, to writers of memoir. Some of what I have to say may be helpful to you; some won't; you'll know what to read and what to skim or skip.

Writing about writing, trying to make sense of this thing you and I do, is a way of getting a little clearer in my own mind (and maybe coming up with something of use to you too) about what happens in stories and novels, how we may improve them, and how we may avoid misery in the process. *The Kite and the String* is the working-out of an idea I've thought about for many years, the idea that writing well doesn't result from following rules and instructions. It comes when we express strong feeling boldly and freely and then look steadily and critically at what we've done, in a mood that's neither despairing nor defensive.

Thinking clearly, you can decide what needs work and what is right as it is. But you may need some help before you can decide: you need some suggestions on what to think about, how to learn from what you read, how to use your agile brain—which gets you through the rest of life—to help you write. And you need some courage—not just courage to write (I see that you're already writing) but courage to write in new ways, to try what may seem intimidating.

This is not a book to pick up if you're trying to work up your nerve to write your first story. (Just write it! You don't need a book!) It's not a how-to manual, and I'm not sure I believe in manuals for writing. This book describes one woman's way of thinking about writing. My imagined audience consists of people who, like me, not only have had the impulse to write stories, but have acted on it repeatedly—enough to have written something or a good many somethings that other people want to read. Or maybe you've mostly accumulated frustrations. Published or not, you aren't a beginner; you've worked at this art.

It's not as easy as it perhaps once was to make a clear distinction between people who are and aren't writers, not when those with multiple responsibilities and little free time (people who earn their living and manage friendship and love, who look after children or frail parents, or who are slowed by their own ill health) write when they can, take it seriously, and may be quite good at it. In this book I'm talking not only to people who have published books or are likely to do so soon, but also to fine writers who may not write much, whose output may consist of a few stories that will be published, with luck, in journals. Writers come in many varieties. They are students in master of fine arts programs, alumni, and those who are considering applying. They are also people who write on their own, maybe showing work to a few friends, as well as those who lead or belong to a workshop at a college, a writers' center, a retirement community, or a friend's house.

I've taught fiction writing to students in master's programs, to undergraduates, to participants in writers' conferences, to people who came to my house once a week for thirteen years to attend a workshop that usually met in my attic; when a wheelchair user joined, we moved to the kitchen. Some of my former students have published well-received books, while others have placed stories in journals, have a lively presence online, teach writing in community colleges, four-year colleges, or universities—or are taking time off from writing to work, look after their kids, or otherwise manage their lives.

The writers I meet have similar difficulties with the task, reasons why this book might be useful. Some are so eager for rules and techniques that they can't allow themselves the many messy stages of writing good fiction, the dreamlike, irrational state of mind that would let them write what's senseless and only later, gradually, turn it into something that makes sense. Others write freely and spontaneously, but have trouble judging what they've done, or thinking in an orderly way about structure or plot. Many lack confidence, and may write less well because they don't have the courage to tell the story they should be telling.

I came to writing fiction late, partly because I didn't know how to start or how to improve but also because I was busy: working, taking care of children, writing what wasn't fiction—interruptions I don't regret. I also had trouble—specifically, an eye ailment.

When I was contemplating writing my first novel, in my late forties (I had written poems and stories), I read John Gardner's *On Becoming a Novelist*, in which the beginning novelist he referred to was always "he" and often "young." We still have remnants of the old idea that a beginning writer is a rough-looking but confident young man who shows up in a class somewhere in a flannel shirt and worn boots, and astonishes the academics with his intense, moving stories. He is forgiven for leaving the practical questions of life to others—primarily a patient wife, who may be supporting him—and when he isn't drinking or riding a motorcycle (or maybe cheating on her), he spends his time writing. My book is for his wife, who always did have a promising manuscript hidden under the dish towels in a kitchen drawer. That is, I assume that my reader (male, female, or other; gay or straight; single or part of a couple) squeezes writing into an ordinary life—one with the usual ties, obligations, interruptions, doubts, and calamities. I can't tell you how to find room in your life for writing (I think you will have to be mildly selfish), but possibly something in my life, or in what I've learned as a writer and teacher, will prove relevant.

I majored in English at Queens College in New York City, to which I commuted by train and bus from my parents' Brooklyn apartment, and graduated in 1962. I went on to study sixteenth- and seventeenth-century literature, chiefly poetry, at Harvard. I thought

I'd be a scholar and write poems in my spare time, but I wasn't good at scholarship, and after graduate school I found a job that excited me more than literary scholarship: teaching expository writing in a community college in Connecticut. I was living in New Haven and newly married to a Yale law student. After we finished our degrees, we moved to Modesto, California, where Edward had been offered a job as a legal aid lawyer in a statewide program that served migrant farmworkers and where I taught in another community college. It was the time of the Vietnam War, and sometimes we drove to San Francisco for peace marches. I had a baby and quit teaching to look after him. Through all those years I thought of myself as a writer— a poet—yet I barely wrote. I had scraps of poems but didn't work on them.

When the baby was four months old, we moved to a tiny house in Sonoma County, under redwood trees, because Edward was now the director of a different office in the same legal aid program. I spent much of the baby's first year breast-feeding in a stained bathrobe or, having managed to take a shower and dress, walking with him in a Gerry pack on my back. I couldn't seem to do much besides care for him, not even laundry. The washer and dryer were in our basement, down a long outdoor staircase. I couldn't leave the baby alone in the house, even asleep, to do laundry, because I wouldn't hear him from the basement. When he was tiny, I put him into the laundry basket on top of the dirty clothes and carried him down there, but at a year he no longer fit into the basket. I finally realized that if I hired a sitter, I could write in the basement— and even do the laundry. I brought my portable typewriter downstairs.

A young woman came for two hours twice a week, and from the basement I heard my son's rapid footsteps over my head. Once, I found a dead mouse in the washing machine and wrote about it in a poem. I did do laundry, but mostly I wrote—and, for the first time in years, stopped feeling guilty for not writing every time I had ten free seconds, because I finally had real writing hours. At the public library I found a list of magazines that published poetry, and I sent poems out; one was accepted. The time in the basement changed me. Writing emerged, dominant, undeniable. I thought that from then on I'd be a serious writer, and I have been.

But with a child, Edward and I wanted to live closer to our families. I wanted to live in a city, where I could put the baby into a stroller and take him to a playground, as my mother had taken me years earlier in Brooklyn. We moved back east and returned to New Haven. Edward again worked as a legal aid lawyer, and I still stayed home. After a few months, when my need to write became intense, we joined a cooperative day care center staffed mostly by parents. By now it was the early seventies, the women's movement was making changes everywhere, and both mothers and fathers were required to work four-hour shifts each week at the center. Our son went to day care for four hours a day, and later his two younger brothers went there as well, so I could write (and, several years later, teach part-time)—a fact that still seems astonishing to me: we put our child into day care though I had earned, so far, $35 from the sale of one poem.

Not that the decision was easy. I was sure people thought I was lazy and self-indulgent: my husband took vacation time every week, and spent it playing with kids and changing diapers at the day care center, so that I could stay home and—of all things—*write poems*. I had no reason to think I'd be a successful writer. It would take three years to publish another poem, and nine years to publish a book of them. Doubtless people did think I was lazy and self-indulgent. I wasn't lazy—writing is hard work—but I was self-indulgent. My husband, in turn, was regarded as heroic, and maybe he was. I think he agreed to join the center out of self-defense, because by then it was clear that I wouldn't be fun to live with if I didn't have writing time. Also, he liked it. He was a shy father, but in the seventies fathers were suddenly expected to participate. The day care center taught him how. People at home with kids ask me regularly how they can write, and I tell them to take advantage of a nice spouse, if they have one, and if not, to look for another way to be a little selfish.

When our youngest son was a baby, I began writing stories. On the strength of the few poems I'd published by then, I had been assigned a creative writing course in the nearby college where I taught English part-time, and since my students would be writing some fiction, I thought I'd better know something about it. Also, I'd had a dream: I was looking over the clothes in a closet, sliding hangers along, and they were actual dresses I'd worn when I was young. Then I turned, and next to the closet was a woman with no head—an omission that in the dream was not surprising or gruesome. She wore a long red plaid dress, a dress I had never owned. She and I embraced, and I knew that in some sense she was I. I woke up. Later that day, raking autumn leaves, I thought, "The dream means I should write fiction." Maybe the woman without a head, in a dress I had never worn, was the "I/not I" who narrates stories: the stranger who emerges from the author's self. Or maybe I was looking for a reason to try a story.

Usually I worked upstairs, but when I sat down to write my first short story—which was about a deaf young man who bakes bread—I put my typewriter on the kitchen table, where the baby was sleeping in a slanting plastic chair. Why he wasn't in his crib I don't know; maybe he'd fallen asleep in his chair and it was simplest to leave him there and stay nearby. Or maybe writing fiction required a different view. That story was never published, but I got some encouraging rejections, and anybody in the business knows how important those are.

For seven years after that, in my thirties and early forties, I wrote both poetry and fiction. I eventually published a collection of poems, but never stopped having trouble publishing individual poems in journals. I couldn't publish fiction—and felt obscurely that it would never be any good until I stopped writing poetry for a time. Finally, in 1983, when I was forty-one, I decided I'd write only poetry in the cold months and only fiction in the warm months. It was spring, and so I wrote fiction first—and it immediately became freer, looser, and more intense. Gradually poetry disappeared—my definition of "the cold months" shortened each year—until finally I no longer had ideas for poems. I had been afraid this would happen, and I minded less than I'd thought I would. Writing is mysterious, and we are stuck with the odd way our particular selves go about it. A couple of years after I began writing fiction exclusively, I began to publish it—first stories, then collections of them, and novels.

Gradually and without knowing what I was up to, I had become a writer of fiction, and writing fiction still dominates my life—a life that (like yours) isn't spent writing fiction all day every day, or writing anything all day every day. Artists' colonies like Yaddo and the MacDowell Colony re-create the freedom bestowed in past times on men who wrote, if they had devoted wives, servants, and either money they had inherited or rare commercial appeal. Most of us, most of the time, must earn money in other ways, often while managing households and children. We stop writing for interruptions good and bad—to celebrate or mourn, to go on vacation or to the hospital. A political movement absorbs our attention; a sick relative needs an advocate; a ceiling falls down. A few months after I began writing fiction exclusively half the year, I discovered a gap in the vision of one eye, which turned out to be caused by a genetic ailment. Since then I've been unable to read with my right eye: anything I look at directly with that eye disappears. I was too young to expect permanent physical loss, and it scared and troubled me. Decades later my eyes are worse, with several other problems, but I can still read, write, and teach; as I age, I'm no longer shocked to have to work around physical limitations.

I've been lucky but also fierce. Selfish. I learned to protect my writing time. But I disagree with those who think writers must protect themselves from *everything*. I have three children and three grandchildren. I want to spend time with friends and family, to do many other things besides write. But I don't know a way to be a professional writer without putting writing ahead of other worthy considerations at times—even though we can't be sure that what we write will be worth reading. It's a gamble we have to make.

The qualities a writer primarily needs, both you and I—not just in order to sit down on the chair but to produce good work—are emotional as much as intellectual. Often the next task is not to learn a technique but to find the courage to use one you already know. New writers speak of the need to find the courage to write, but once they've shown up at an MFA program or a writers' conference or even just that coffee shop, they may think that the emotional work is done and they can now follow prescribed rules and procedures to make up characters and the rest, if only they can find out what those rules are.

Writers must be at peace with the process, so they trust themselves when they come up with an idea for the next scene—which may well turn out to be wrong, but which may suggest something right. We need the courage to waste time, even though we have so little of it. It takes time to discern what's obscured in the dark at the back of the mind, but is what the piece needs—but often we won't have much of an answer if we're asked if we've accomplished anything.

People sometimes ask, skeptically, if it's really possible to teach someone to write. They seem to think that those who have the impulse ought to be able to figure out the rest on their own—and if they can't, they're just not writers. But all the writers I know have learned something essential from some kind of teaching, whether in classes, in informal groups, from reviews, or from books. We learn, if not what to do next, how to start thinking about it. In *The Kite and the String*, I hope to help you think about your writing, and to approach the task with more confidence, excitement, and hope.

PART I

The Kite and the String

CHAPTER 1

Writing with Freedom and Common Sense

The Sound of Storytelling

Plenty of people—most people—don't write stories and don't want to. A few keep saying that one of these days they will write a story, a novel, or a memoir, implying that this task will be simple once they get around to it. That leaves those of us who regularly fool around—or make ourselves miserable—with sentences in which an imaginary person—or a real or sort of real person whom, at present, we are imagining does something, sentences like "I opened the door." Or maybe, we decide, "The door, as I opened it . . ." or "Opening—in a hurry—the door . . ."

We may not remember how this odd practice began—putting human beings on the page and making them suffer and fear, making them love, discovering that they are about to do something we never thought they might. Like sexual longing, the wish to write—to make any art—starts in the body and precedes coherent thought about it. We want to hold a pen, or to type. Our fingers tingle; they are full of words. We have an itch, a yen, and the world tells us what our desire is called and whether it's one of the allowable kinds of wanting in our particular culture. Writing is closer to sex than we sometimes think, and for the susceptible, making sentences they like, at least for the moment ("Trembling, I opened the door, and just outside . . .") may induce arousal. Making up—or remembering—story is alluring and dangerous, even subversive: although writing is legal, it's disturbing to people uncomfortable with the ownership of an imagination, and some will do all they can to keep us from it, even if we are people they love. Writers of fiction and memoir, more than writers of fact, must defend—sometimes fiercely—their art and the time they give it. (And it's even worse for poets.)

As shocking as narrative—writing that tells a story—may be, however, this is a book about it, about those phrases and sentences we fret over ("Until I had opened the door . . ."). Fiction—sheer invention—may be most unsettling to unimaginative people: the lifelike nature of unreal people can be downright alarming. But the process of writing memoir isn't so different. When the memory comes, or the realization comes—"Here I must write down what Uncle Steve did!"—it is almost as surprising to the writer, as mysterious, as it would be if Uncle Steve weren't real.

Even before we want to make up narrative, we may find we love the sound and feel of story, its texture against our minds. As a college freshman I read James Joyce's story "A Painful Case." The main character, Mr. Duffy, is a Dublin bachelor who writes, adding sentences now and then to a manuscript that we sense goes nowhere. He is incurably lonely: when he makes a friend, he becomes so frightened that he ends the connection, and the story is about his belated understanding that his withdrawal was wrong and harmful. He is not someone to emulate, except possibly for his moment of insight at the end. But at the beginning of the story, we learn that he "had an odd autobiographical habit which led him to compose in his mind from time to time a short sentence about himself containing a subject in the third person and a predicate in the past tense," and when I first read this story, I was more struck by that sentence than by anything else. I too composed such sentences, also in the third-person past tense. I secretly narrated parts of my life to myself, as if I lived in the unexciting parts of a novel, the transitions in which characters get dressed or walk to the bus stop. Like a child realizing that others have heard of masturbation and even named it, I was amazed to learn that anyone else had this "odd autobiographical habit" or knew about it, and I wondered if Joyce had it too—if it meant I might be a writer. I've since discovered that when I mention my own reaction to that sentence to other writers, many will smile, flushing with pleasure and self-consciousness.

Maybe Mr. Duffy's sentences are "short" because he's ambivalent about his imagination; perhaps Joyce meant that Mr. Duffy sticks to simple facts when he narrates his life to himself, and the sentences he thinks are something like "He ate his dinner." He's a rigid person who can't let himself live the freer life he is drawn to. For better or worse, my inward sentences, when I was a child, weren't short or truthful. "She carried the plate from the cupboard," I might begin, but then I'd go on, giving my life an old-fashioned, literary flavor, "and gently set the simple earthenware dish with its chipped glaze on the scarred wooden table"—revising my mother's Danish Modern stoneware and Formica-topped aluminum kitchen set.

Whatever Mr. Duffy used his "odd autobiographical habit" for, I told my life to myself to pretend I was not just writing or reading a novel, but *in one*: I gave myself a narrated life. I think I wanted my actual life to be describable in the way that fictional lives may be described: I wanted it to suit the alert, androgynous, slightly acid tone of a sympathetic but sharp-eyed narrator, moral yet subtle, who observes and presents characters who may be flawed and confused but are worthy of our attention. It's a tone perfected in the British Isles, especially toward the end of the nineteenth century and in the first decades of the twentieth:

> For a minute or two she stood looking at the house, and wondering what to do next, when suddenly a footman in livery came running out of the wood—(she considered him to be a footman because he was in livery: otherwise, judging by his face only, she would have called him a fish)—and rapped loudly at the door with his knuckles.
>
> —from *Alice's Adventures in Wonderland*, by Lewis Carroll, 1865

> At lunch her brother, seeing her inclined for silence, insisted on talking. Tibby was not ill-natured, but from babyhood something drove him to do the unwelcome and the unexpected. Now he gave her a long account of the day-school that he sometimes patronised. The account was interesting, and she had often pressed him for it before, but she could not attend now, for her mind was focussed on the invisible.
>
> —from *Howards End*, by E. M. Forster, 1910

> Running below the beat and braying of the music was the steady needle-scratch on the gramophone record. Each sound had another underlying sound. She felt that if she could concentrate she would unpeel the outer sounds from the inner one, the one now buried, the last sound before complete silence—the tick of the blood in

her wrist, she thought, turning her hand on the chair; the
voice of her own mind.

—from *A Game of Hide and Seek*, by Elizabeth Taylor, 1951

When I began writing fiction I had no idea how to do it. I loved
fiction's capacity to depict subtle shifts in awareness and scrupulous ethical distinctions; action without interior life had no lure.
However, *all* I had was my love of how narrative can reveal the
inner life. Even after writing poems, after studying literature, after
making up narrative sentences like Joyce's Mr. Duffy, I was stuck.
I had no subject matter, no ready tales to tell. I hadn't lived much—
hadn't been a bartender or a taxi driver or a merchant marine. I'd
been a student, a camp counselor, a teacher, and a mother. One
summer I'd been a salesclerk at Macy's. It would take me years to
have the nerve to fake what I hadn't experienced.

My education wasn't bad for a writer. I had learned to think
about words, to hear their sounds. I wouldn't forget that writing is
composed of words, not feeling or experience. And I didn't make
the mistake some new writers make, imagining that if something
worth writing about happened at 2 p.m. on Monday, the words that
come to mind somehow *are* "2 p.m. on Monday," that the event has
been reproduced, so if a reader says, "This doesn't seem real," the
writer can say smugly, "But it happened."

I knew about words, and a few other things. I knew that writing
must be ambitious if it is to be any good: it must concern itself with
what matters most. And I knew that often the sharply observed,
objective detail, presented with understatement and maybe even
irony, can convey feeling at least as effectively as the effusive
abstract outburst.

But though I'd read plenty of it, I had failed to notice what narrative was. What I loved most—the inner life on the page—was

real, at least in stories that centered on character rather than action, which would inevitably be the kind I'd prefer. But I hadn't noticed that narrative is not *just* about interior life, that even when the action in a story, novel, or memoir would not interest a police officer or a military strategist, it is still action. The genius of narrative is not just to describe interior states but to embody them—to find an equivalent for them in the visible world. A woman who, in real life, might simply think envious thoughts about a friend's good fortune, in a story drops the coveted valuable object down a storm drain, and the moment when she pauses to flick her hair off her face, loosening her grip on the borrowed antique silver bracelet, makes us know and feel her rage. The novelist may invent the dropping of the bracelet; the memoirist may recall something that happened, something that will represent the emotion. All the inwardness that I loved notwithstanding, narrative is first (not always, of course) about the tangible.

But for years my characters did little more than think and feel. It had taken me decades to stop focusing on myself and be interested enough in other people to invent characters at all. Learning to play in the world, to use its capacities when I made up story, came still more slowly.

Also, I didn't know what a contemporary story might be like. However much I loved James Joyce and Henry James, as a late-twentieth-century Jewish woman from Brooklyn, I wouldn't write stories that sounded like theirs. I'd read little contemporary fiction and almost no stories or autobiographical essays; I believed that short stories were intellectual exercises with little surprises at the end that I wouldn't know how to come up with. Now, decades later, I learn each time I read Joyce's, James's, or any other good writer's stories, but then I needed models I could connect to more directly. Nowadays I often suggest that students read writers who have written about the places where they grew up, or the ethnic group they belong to, or the kind of life they've led—immigrant life, for example. It's important to read widely and deeply, all kinds of books—but it's also important to realize (it may come as a shock) that your own neighborhood and history, the particular way your aunt cooked vegetables, could go into your writing. Don't limit yourself to your own experience ("Write what you know" is only sometimes good advice; "Write what you don't know" is equally good)—but don't assume that your own experience is too humble and boring for fiction.

As for me, browsing in bookstores, I at last came upon the stories of Tillie Olsen and Grace Paley. And in them ordinary people—urban women, sometimes urban Jewish feminist women like me—managed their lives despite the difficulties caused by ambivalence, divided loyalties, moral quandaries, and inner contradiction, not to mention poverty, prejudice, war, and the inevitable conflicts between private life and life in society. Maybe things did happen, after all, in lives like the ones I knew. Seeing that stories could talk about what mattered to me—to a woman with kids, a woman past first youth, an urban American woman—was the first step toward finding tone and subject matter.

Controlled Daydreaming

Writing anything—even if it's rational and factual—involves guesswork, intuition, and imagination. Something indefinable tells the journalist to talk to the short soldier before approaching the tall one; hunches guide the writer of science or history.

Memoirists must also make choices they can't always explain about when to begin, what to emphasize, whom to leave out. The fiction writer, in addition, has the freedom to create people and events out of nothing, whether part of a story comes from life or not. Even when fiction writers start from a real incident, we change endings, compress people and events, and make up what we don't remember. The imaginative possibilities when you haven't sworn to tell the truth and nothing but the truth are dazzling. The essence of fiction is not that it isn't true but that it *might* not be true: it's a house with an open back door into which anything may come ("I opened the *back door* . . .").

The writer of fiction must be on particularly friendly terms with the unpredictable, welcoming the illogical way ideas come, the painful and embarrassing thoughts that pass through an unguarded mind.

Setting out to write narrative, whether it's fiction or memoir, we make an agreement with ourselves to live—in part—irrationally, to honor impulse and hunches. We must follow whatever route leads us to the unprotected part of the self, from which good writing comes. And whatever we discover about the writing we do, we must never let ourselves confuse it with something accessible to directions and rules and methodologies.

But if good writing is mysterious, illogical, and contradictory—if it comes from what's most essential and un-sorted-out in our minds—then how is it possible for us to learn how to produce it or to help others learn? We don't want to kill it with methods and rules, but the solution can't be to wait for inspiration, to proceed haphazardly. We've all met writers who do that—"I just write from my heart," they say—and it leads to cliché and formlessness. A few people write well without much effort, but I am not one of them, and you may not be either.

~

My own experience may prove useful here. I learned much of what I know from my parents—who weren't storytellers. They did read to my sister and me, and my mother read novels and plays for pleasure; I grew up—no small thing—assuming that reading was desirable. Reading, yes, but not allowing the strangeness and mystery in books to encroach on ordinary life. I picture my mother stepping down a grassy slope from a rented cabin in a tidy bungalow colony in the eastern Adirondacks to a mountain lake. Her white terry cloth beach jacket is open over her ruched bathing suit, which rarely gets wet. A folding chair is under one arm, and in her other hand is her knitting bag, with a thick novel by Edna Ferber sticking out of it next to her cigarettes. At the beach she may tell a friend a story, but her stories could all be summed up as "I thought the bus would be on time—but it was late!" or "I thought the bus would be late—but it was on time!"

My father—curly hair that went gray early; dark, emphatic eyebrows; a bare, skinny torso; baggy bathing trunks—stands at the edge of the water. He's bouncing on the balls of his feet, leading up to one of his long, slow swims; he swam a lopsided one-armed overhand stroke he invented, disappearing entirely when the active arm was underwater. He was an eccentric, and though he'd have denied it, a man of intense feeling. Now he's talking to someone, gesturing vigorously, his voice so loud he sounds angry. *His* stories could all be titled "That's Ridiculous!" A bank, a store, the government, a child—or maybe the friend to whom he is speaking—had failed, failed at something.

When I grew up, I began handing my mother the novels I read, and she read them but described tamer books than I knew. Once, I gave her Henry Roth's *Call It Sleep*, about Jewish immigrants in New York, living much as her own parents had lived. She phoned to tell me she had enjoyed it.

"A lot of Oedipal stuff in that book," I said—showing off, thinking of the passionately connected mother and son.

"Oh, I *know*!" said my mother, who didn't hear well by then. "Pot roast! Noodles!" Edible stuff.

They were conscientious parents, loving parents, if not particularly self-aware. Above all they believed in common sense, and my sister once characterized my mother's philosophy as "If a thought is not rational, rational people do not think it." What I learned about ambivalence and emotional complexity, I learned from books or from my own rebellious mind. From my parents I learned that if you just did what made sense, things would work out—unless you were dealing with a *tragedy*, of course. Death, for example—of a person (not a dog), of a *nice* person—might be a reason to cry, but a daughter who cried when the high school student newspaper printed a banner headline announcing her grade point average, the highest in the school that term, was being silly. A high average was *good*, and having everyone know about it was even better, certainly nothing to cry about! I grew up knowing there was something about life that my parents would never recognize and that I would never be able to ignore—and that I had to do something about this; maybe that's why I became a writer in the first place.

But on ordinary occasions, when the high school newspaper wasn't making everybody hate me forever, I learned—how could I not?—my parents' way of thinking, and became (most of the time) a predictable and sensible, if mildly boring, woman, someone who still follows instructions and does what she's supposed to do on time, making lists and taking pleasure in crossing items off. Common sense made me unexciting but competent. Raising three children helped too. I cooked too much spaghetti and scraped too many carrots to take myself particularly seriously. When the *New Yorker*, astonishingly, began printing my fiction, I continued to supervise homework and fold laundry, feed dogs and cats and children. In most respects I was the woman my parents had hoped I'd be, though they might have preferred someone who took fewer emotional risks. They were proud of my work, if nervous around it, and my mother used to go into bookstores and turn my books to face front.

I grew up sensible, yet I knew that a more surprising, less easily explained territory might be mine—might, in fact, belong with my need to look at paintings in museums and my comfort in ambivalence, in people who confessed to inappropriate feelings, as my feelings were often inappropriate. One aunt told true stories out of her life, in which the unexpected always happened, chaos was inches away, the villains were heroic and vice versa, and you had to move fast, because—she seemed to know—soon enough would come despair. When I was young, she lived around the corner with her family and half a dozen German shepherds. I'd ring her bell, stroke the dogs, who pressed their firm bodies into mine, and install myself in a corner of her kitchen, listening and watching while Aunt Clare cooked dog food from scratch and recounted her week. My mother (her older sister) loved and deplored her.

Yet even my mother told an unforgettable story a few times, in the same matter-of-fact voice she used for her stories about the bus. One was a few sentences long: An aunt of hers had an illegitimate child back in Europe, and the child was adopted by religious relatives. Grown, the girl announced to the woman she thought was her birth mother that she planned to marry a man who wasn't Jewish, and the adoptive mother said, shockingly, "I am not your mother." I turned this account into a thirty-page story. When I showed it to my mother, she said, "Something like this happened in my family." She didn't remember telling me.

My father occasionally told stories of his youth—of being sent on a boat to Rhode Island as a seven-year-old, to stay with relatives during the flu epidemic of 1918; of playing in a jazz band in the Catskills in the 1930s, and what happened when the owner of the resort could no longer pay them. My father knew that uncertainty could be exciting or charming, but mostly he denied that. If I looked hard, there was evidence that common sense wasn't everything, that even my sober parents didn't think it was *everything*.

Most of the time, however, my parents were firm: there was *no such thing* as the irrational, nothing so special that it merited the kind of fuss some people made. They were secular Jews who didn't believe in souls or religion, and considered nothing sacred except maybe Franklin D. Roosevelt. They weren't homophobic, racist, or particularly sexist—not because they had broken through prejudice but because they didn't start by clinging to a set of beliefs, except that my mother believed that children should wear undershirts and that people given presents should send thank-you notes. If the lesbian couple in their apartment building had failed to send thank-you notes—well, *that* would be worthy of disapproval! My mother was a teacher of homebound children, the "physically handicapped," they were called then. Teaching sick or disabled kids in their houses, she was as matter-of-fact with them and their parents, as calm about their problems, as she was about everything else. Disabled children should also write thank-you notes.

Maybe the double awareness I developed—"There is no such thing as irrepressible, irrational, intense feeling/There is nothing else"—not only made me a writer (I had to say I had the feelings I was being told nobody had), but also, when I got around to writing fiction, eventually taught me how to do it. By keeping hold of both contradictory states of awareness—intense feeling and common sense—I could create stories that had some modicum of interest, because the feeling was real, and I could figure out how to make them better. I needed abandon and control—a kite that takes off into the wind, a restraining string that's unspooled a little at a time and pulled when necessary, a string that lets it fly, but not so far that it gets lost.

"Well, what *ought* to work?" I'd think, and still do. Letting the unexpected come, then reasoning things through, letting loose again and reasoning again, remains my way of working, and is what I urge my students to try. Because of the haphazard process by which I learned to write fiction, when I need to solve a problem in my own work, I figure out, haltingly (belatedly realizing that the answer is much like what I figured out last time), something that writers elsewhere have a name and a procedure for. I think this is good.

"I *understand!*" a new student told me impatiently, after a discussion of her story. "I need to work on *character development* and *point of view.*" No, she needed to turn herself into one of the people in her story and feel what the character felt, become a fool in the way the character was a fool. Students talk about "point of view" or even, in writing about it, "pov," as if it were mechanical, when in fact it refers to the hardest and most thrilling thing we do —becoming someone else, becoming that person so thoroughly that if we've decided the person is nearsighted, we'll imagine the room in a blur as soon as she takes off her glasses; if we've made him so jealous he can kill, we'll feel mad rage down to our tingling fingertips when his girlfriend looks at another man.

I need more words than my students do to say how I write, and I think that's a benefit. I'd rather think of "other things that might be going on in the characters' lives," for example, than "subplots,"

a word that doesn't help me make up story. Characters are insepa-
rable (it seems to me) from what they do. I know that discussions
of writing often focus on "characters" and then "plot," but in this
book we'll do something different: we'll consider first what goes
into a narrative—events and the people involved in them—and
then how we make coherent, aesthetically complete shapes out of
the subject matter we've dreamed up. Throughout, the process
will prove to be emotional as much as intellectual: often the problem is not what to do but how to find the nerve to do it.

When I began writing fiction, I had a love of words, feeling, and the
inheritance I couldn't shake—common sense. Now I think that is a
good set of tools. It doesn't work to write a story in clichés and gen-
eralities, to postpone fixing up the language until the last draft: the
story's meaning is in its language, and it has no existence without
language. We need specific verbs and nouns, accurate adverbs and
adjectives, no vague metaphors or clichés. As for feeling and common sense, we must learn to entertain them in rapid succession.
There are times for letting loose, letting ideas come freely, without
permitting ourselves or others to criticize, and at such times it's
important to banish the internal critic, to become so "sleepy and
stupid"—as Lewis Carroll describes Alice just before she sees the
White Rabbit—that thoughts and convergences we'd dismiss if we
were fully awake can find their way onto the page. When we judge
too quickly, we censor ourselves, writing nothing, or what's unob-
jectionable but lifeless. We must slowly learn to drop our inhibitions
when we write. Keeping what we produce secret for a time may
make that easier. If we assure ourselves that before showing anyone
what we're writing, we'll get rid of what would embarrass us or
make others angry, we can keep the offending passages for the time

being—and, keeping them, we may get used to them, and decide they are worth our embarrassment or others' anger (and often, when our writing does make people angry, it's not for the reasons we expected).

There are also times for looking over and thinking about what we've written, setting our critical intelligence loose. We must make sure the writing is clear and not repetitious, that the story arrives somewhere. We'll pay most attention, at such times, not to what makes writing great but to what makes it possible: what makes it whole and coherent. Periodically we'll need to banish the critic again, become sleepy and stupid again, and let new ideas come to mind.

People who write freely but don't stop and think may get down on paper scraps of the intensity of life, but what they write, in a fever, is not necessarily clear, not shaped, not given point and direction. It's repetitious or it leaves out something essential. Its beauty, if it has beauty, may be spoiled by cliché or self-absorption. Strong feeling without common sense makes amateurs who may express what they feel to their own satisfaction, but can't turn it into something a reader can take pleasure in.

But writing without heartache and joy, though it may be more orderly, is worse. People who write without strong feeling don't really use common sense either. Common sense tells us that when we write, we are always taking a risk, describing people in trouble or potential trouble because *we* have been in trouble, or at least have known and feared trouble, known that nobody is ever certifiably safe. Without that knowledge—without a clear awareness that we write, that we make any art, because life is joyfully tragic and solemnly comic all at once—why would we bother?

Yet people do bother without strong feeling, producing what they hope is art, but risking little and even avoiding the heartache of writing itself—the fear we all experience when we see how hard writing is, how unlikely any of us is to do it well with any consistency. Students turn up in MFA programs or writing classes prepared to work hard, learn, reason—but not to cry, not to write as the whole human beings they inevitably are; that is, people who have felt rage, shame, and fear. There are no rules or directions for making up characters and putting them into exciting situations. Everybody who can read and write can just do it, and then use common sense to try to figure out how to do it better.

Common sense will tell us plenty. It tells us when enough is enough, for example. Students who rely on "craft" have been told, "Show, don't tell," and rarely think, "Hey, isn't there a point at which one should tell, not show?" And of course there is. "Showing"—describing in concrete, specific, objective language—is essential to much narrative writing, but there comes a time to say, "She was ten years old" or "I didn't like the restaurant" or "It was a lousy time in their marriage." Common sense tells us when something is a good idea and when it's no longer a good idea. The opposite of every rule is sometimes true. Writers don't need rules as much as we need the freedom to take risks and to make simple decisions for simple, practical reasons—much like the workaday, unglamorous decisions we make in ordinary life. If a piece of writing—that all-important sheet of paper with black marks on it—is a kite that the strong winds of feeling are blowing across the sky, we need a string to grasp. We need freedom above all, but we also need control.

PART II

People Taking Action

CHAPTER 2

Imagine

One of my grandsons, at five, told me that a spider's web is "the strongest thing in the *whole wide world*." A few days later I found myself watching a small yellowish spider climbing the back of a wooden kitchen chair. It went up a few inches, then detached itself from the chair—or lost touch with the chair—and swayed in the air for a while, hanging by a filament of web, with its legs gathered in so it looked like a withered flower. It climbed again, then hung again. The spider supported its weight with something it had created out of its own insides—as if you or I could spit on a nearby object and then support our bodies in the air, swinging from a string of saliva. Clearly, a spider's web is the strongest thing in the whole wide world. Except for the writer's imagination, on which it is also possible to suspend your entire weight.

"Where do you get your ideas?" audience members ask plaintively at bookstore readings. Some sound genuinely baffled or even resentful: how does this happen, they want to know (and why doesn't it happen to me?).

The question makes me feel slightly accused, and indeed, as we've said, there is something frightening about your mind's capacity to invent people doing things and then to bring them to life for the reader: to make a reader cry when an imagined person dies; to make her love people who never existed; or to bring into the room your mother, who is thousands of miles away, or dead— and to tell secrets about her, or at least to tell what feel like secrets about a person who might possibly be your mother.

Making up story out of nothing is something like trafficking in the occult. In *A Midsummer Night's Dream*, Shakespeare has Theseus condemn imagination, which is common to "the lunatic, the lover, and the poet." He says:

> The poet's eye, in a fine frenzy rolling,
> Doth glance from heaven to earth, from earth to heaven;
> And as imagination bodies forth
> The forms of things unknown, the poet's pen
> Turns them to shapes, and gives to airy nothing
> A local habitation and a name.

> (5.1.12–18)

Who has the right to do *that*? But right or wrong, we do it, and the real question is how. This is a chapter about invention: why I think you should cherish and nurture your capacity to make things up, and how you might go about that.

Students I work with are often (this continues to surprise me) afraid to imagine. When I teach fiction, I assume that what is turned in is invented and doesn't have much to do with a student's life, though I'm not surprised when a story takes place in the city where the writer lives or concerns people who do her kind of work. But surely (I invariably think) the people and what happens to them are made up—why else would she have enrolled in a fiction program? Yet time and again, after congratulating my student on the wonderful character she's created—the protagonist's husband, let's say, who limps after a childhood accident, plays the bagpipes (and goes in for kinky sex)—I find myself shaking hands after graduation with a friendly man who leans on a cane and wears a T-shirt commemorating a recent bagpipe festival. What is going on here?

Of course, bits of life turn up in fiction—haphazardly, by accident. Starting a novel, I once lay down on my bed determined not to stand up until I knew what a character's husband was obsessed with, so I'd know what kind of trouble a troublesome old woman might have gotten into in her youth. After a while I thought, "Trolleys." With that idea, I looked up trolleys in the 1920s, found that I should say "streetcars," and learned that the trouble was strikes. I wrote a novel.

Later I noticed a ticket with a picture of an old-fashioned streetcar on my dresser. I'd kept it from a trip to Charleston, South Carolina, where you could travel through the historic downtown on a bus that looked like a streetcar. Had a glance at the ticket made me think of trolleys? Maybe. But I didn't start by looking at the ticket and figuring out what I thought about Charleston and how that might become a story.

There's nothing *wrong* with basing fiction on your life, either changing it just enough to keep your relatives from getting mad, changing it quite a bit—or not changing it at all. Or you can put in a few completely fictional elements, call the piece "autofiction," and tease the reader, who (at least this is the theory, I gather) will be titillated by the knowledge that some of the story is true and some is untrue, and it's impossible to know which is which. All these practices can lead to fine fiction. But often I suspect that because there's nothing *wrong* with writing fiction about your life, my students assume that their lives will be the *only* source for their fiction, that everything will arise from something real. I think writing a lot of fiction based on what's true makes us timid and conservative.

When I teach fiction workshops, I don't let students talk about the possibly autobiographical origins of their stories, so as to leave me the freedom to say, "This mother comes across as an appalling person," without insulting my student's actual mother, at least in so many words. Or that's what I claim when I interrupt students as they're saying, "This is based . . ." Part of my real reason is that I believe (perhaps foolishly) that by talking about the piece as if it's fiction, I will make it more likely that my student will *write* fiction, will make it more fictional. I want more fiction, and I urge students to make things up, because I've come to believe that some of them, at least, are basing their stories on what really happened not because of an aesthetic principle I have no right to question, but because they are afraid to make things up or think they can't.

I don't care if your story is based on your life, if writing it doesn't make you that much more reluctant to write an invented story next, and if I don't have to hear about how it resembles what actually occurred. And if your story *is* based on life, don't simply change your mother's name and then picture your mother as you write. Invent some details about your fictional character that make it impossible for that person to look like your actual relative, and get yourself into the habit of picturing the character, not the person who inspired her. If your story was originally about a real-life person called Louise, whom you're now calling Babette, stop yourself from thinking about "Louise" and picturing Louise's actual house and actual turned-up nose. Give Babette a different house and a different nose, and maybe she'll do something that Louise would never have done, but that will make for a better story.

In that way you'll be able to drop the feeling that you're some-how writing this story *for* Louise, or to get revenge on Louise, or to understand Louise. Make the story loyal to the story, not to the facts that gave you the idea.

I'd rather read memoir that's identified as memoir and fiction that is identified as fiction and—even if it isn't entirely invented—has renounced any claim to represent what actually happened, has given up trying to be faithful to Grandpa's memory or the family's tragedy or what went wrong when the marriage failed. I want invention to take place as the story demands it, not as history demands it: if Grandpa turns out to be a force for evil in the story, so be it. The story comes first, and I think that's a grand opportu-nity, a huge source of fun, and a challenge we would be foolish to reject. And your writing won't betray you about what's important. That is, if you write the story openly and honestly, it will reflect what you actually think of your grandfather—though it may not correspond to the family myth about him.

Besides, your real mother—or grandfather—is three-dimensional and alive and has a history it would take twenty volumes to get down in full, while the character on the page is a short series of black letters, so—no matter what you intend and no matter how talented you are—what's on the page can't possibly represent your unpredict-able, maddening, lovable, crazy mother or your mysterious grandfa-ther. So if you're a fiction writer, one of these days write some memoir and try to get your actual relative onto the page, insofar as that's possible. If you write memoir, you've probably discovered already that it too, inevitably, is about invented characters.

Life will only rarely inspire complete, good stories, though it offers endless *moments* that may *contribute to* a story. So if you're going to learn to write fiction, you'd better get in the habit of inventing material when life doesn't provide it. How many novels can you write about husbands who play the bagpipes? And if you're a memoirist, better look around for factual stories that don't involve your own life. Sooner or later, unless you've lived a particularly long and adventurous one, you'll use it up.

There's another reason why depending too much on autobiography can be a bad idea. You know too well what the point of your own stories is. "There goes Dad," you think, "knowing yet again how to damage my self-respect," or "Yup, she asked that question only because I'm black." You may well be right, but knowing the theme of the story before you begin makes for a predigested story, one that will be obvious to you and your readers too soon. Writing well involves surprising ourselves, giving what we don't yet know we care about a chance to emerge. Good writing goes through stages in which it's not so good. In the first few drafts of a new story, there may be no apparent theme; the reason for writing about this subject isn't yet clear. Only slowly do we realize what a story is about. If, when writing fiction, you make yourself write a story that didn't happen—instead of just writing a story about what did happen except that you call a writing class an art class—then you'll have a chance to learn. Writing fact, look for a topic on which you're not already an expert. Incidents and their consequences may lead you to grasp something you never thought of before. Good writing comes when we risk not knowing what we're doing—struggling, surprising ourselves, thinking through something that makes us uncomfortable.

A student of mine wrote a terrific story, and I was excited because he'd been having trouble with the idea that stories need action that leads somewhere, that stories turn on event. In his new story, indeed, a significant event (the main character found out that something about himself was known to others, though he had thought it was a secret) brought the character's feelings to a climax.

Later I heard that what happened in the story was pretty much what had happened in the writer's real life, and I felt disappointed and wondered why I felt that—after all, despite my wish that my students would do more inventing, there really isn't anything wrong with basing good fiction on real life. Eventually I realized that I had thought this man had finally understood how to think up a climactic moment. But apparently he'd *experienced* a climactic moment. I was moved and surprised by the big event in his story, but he already knew about it. Life had offered him a story, but it may not have helped him understand what he needed to learn about writing fiction.

Another student had many uncertainties about her life, and as she put it, all her stories were about a young woman "who can't make decisions." When she pushed herself to make up stories about people who were not like her and whose problems didn't resemble her problems, she revealed a great imaginative range and empathy. It was as if she had thought she had to figure out her life before she could write stories—and once she looked in a different direction on purpose, all sorts of ideas came. It's not that the new stories were outlandish. If I hadn't known her age and a few facts about her, I wouldn't have known whether the new stories were autobiographical or not. Like her old stories, they were nuanced, observant, emotionally sharp—but they weren't all about the same person. She was suddenly putting herself into the minds of people who were older than she was, or who were men, or who were in a circumstance she'd never been in. Ideas came.

Invention is inevitably the central act in writing fiction, whether it's inventing people and actions from nothing, or inventing slight deviations from factual truth: conversations, time sequences, weather. We're already doing it. But we can perhaps learn to do it more easily and more often. When writing fiction, we may start with something true and add something else that's factually true, or something invented, to complete a story. But we may also start with what's invented and add something else invented. Like the little yellow spider hanging from the back of my kitchen chair, we make something out of nothing, trust it to hold the story up, and then make something more. I think it may be the strangeness of that idea—the spider doesn't fall down—that keeps some students I work with from inventing. Surely an entire story—or novel—can't arise from the imagination? Can the mind actually do this? Yes.

What makes a story *good* is that—even if we don't understand what we're doing as we write—what happens in it corresponds in some way to what's most intense in us. We may invent the people and actions, but we've felt the emotions. We write because there is something *unspeakable*—something we should not say, or cannot explain in words. And the story—the events in the story, the content—gives words to the unspeakable. Strong feeling, like it or not, marks every life. That's our source. But because it's strong, at ordinary times we'd rather not feel it, and we may hide from ourselves the knowledge that we have ever felt it—knowledge of our desire, anger, and fear.

Invention comes about when we allow it to happen. Depending on how comfortable you are with what's shocking, how much of an exhibitionist you are, you may or may not have to work hard to learn what's in your imagination. If you're one of those for whom it's difficult to be naked on the page, you may find yourself writing what doesn't matter much, or writing to the right and left of a story, avoiding the central, intense event. It's helpful, when you're in search of a story, to think of yourself as two people: the one who wants to write it and the one who is shocked by its connection to your own feelings, and would rather keep it hidden. The goal is to distract and soothe the censor, so the blurter can blurt.

How can you make things up if ideas don't come? It's not as hard as some people think. The point is to look out for things that occur in the tangible world, and have tangible results—that don't merely alter someone's feelings. Say you've made your character Babette say something hurtful to a guest, and you're about to follow it with three pages telling us how bad the guest feels. Instead, what if you skip the description of the guest's hurt feelings and tell us what she does? Perhaps—insulted—she leaves Babette's house and then must stay at the only hotel in town, where she can't pay the bill and must ask Babette to bail her out. And *then* what will happen? Ask yourself what *could* happen in your character's situation—what could complicate matters?—and make a list of many bad ideas that may turn out to include a good idea. A student of mine was thinking about a story in which two estranged family members would meet at a wedding—and something would change between them. How to make it happen? When we began to talk about what could go wrong at a wedding, she saw what to do: some mishap could force the estranged people to confront each other, or to do something together, or just to speak. We started listing possible helpful catastrophes: the bride decides not to get married, the groom has a fight with the bride's father, the caterer is late, the champagne punch spills, the photographer . . . You get the idea. If you think of several possible incidents, one may feel right—emotionally right— and capable of leading to another action or event. In the ensuing complexity your characters will be able to express what is in them. Try that one. You can always try another.

Stimulate your mind with what's arbitrary. You may think of the next scene in your story if you tell yourself that it will involve an object that starts with the letter "m." Play games in which you arbitrarily choose something to write about: a newspaper story, a word you land on by chance in the dictionary, a phrase overheard.

If you don't get ideas, it may be helpful to leave your desk, to go somewhere where you feel more anonymous, whether you are or not. Write nonsense for a while. Make notes of what goes through your mind, whether the notes seem useful or don't. Looking at paintings or sculpture, listening to music, can also free the mind. Go to a concert or an art gallery. Or go to a place where you can look at people—a supermarket will do if you don't live in a neighborhood where people walk around. Watch people until— this is important—the right ones come along. They will be in a group of at least two, and they will have a certain look, a certain presence to your eye (though they might not catch anyone else's eye), that will make it possible to imagine that they are at an important moment in their lives. Watch them for a while. Go home, choose the one from whose viewpoint you will write, and write a paragraph that makes clear how they are connected, why they are where you saw them, and what the character in whose mind you've landed wants right now, or is afraid may happen. You don't know anything about them, so you must invent—but arbitrarily restricting yourself to what's possible, given what you do know, may be stimulating. If you see a woman in her twenties with a small child, you may decide she is not the child's mother but his aunt or teacher or even kidnapper, but she can't be his grandmother; she's too young. I suppose she can be his step-grandmother, married to his much older grandfather. Part of what makes this exercise work is that it's ethically suspect to go around staring at people. Writing is often ethically suspect, but wrongdoing is stimulating.

If you don't want to go out in the rain or to be bad, imagine two people coming out of a building, and then ask yourself questions about them—are they glad to be coming out of the building, or would they rather stay inside? Are they about to separate, or will they stay together? Is *that* what they want? *Both* of them? Postpone, for a while, questions like "How old are they?" First ask questions that will make you know what matters intensely to them. Only then will you focus on age, sex, where they are, and what exactly they are looking forward to or fearing.

You can devise your own ways of coming up with subject matter. Anything illogical will do. The point is to get yourself into the habit of paying attention to fleeting thoughts and emotions, objects or people you have noticed, and then finding, from the possible subjects around all of us, one that holds your attention. You may end up writing about your own life after all, or a version of it, but you'll come at it through the unpredictable and unmapped precincts of the chaotic inner life.

Invention comes about when we let it, when we don't mind feeling stupid as we do it—it feels like what children do; it *is* what children do—when we clear a place for it, become quiet, and wait. When you are in touch with your characters, you'll eventually think of the event that rightly concludes their story (but it may require hours of patient or impatient doodling).

Sometimes the incident you want will come from outside the character's life—not a deus ex machina that solves or ruins everything, but an ordinary event that, coming right when it does (a phone call in the middle of the marriage proposal, a child's minor accident at the moment of misunderstanding), changes everything.

At other times the incident will emerge, like the spider's web, from what you've already made. Stare hard at what you've written, and see what isn't yet there. What object does the character have with her—must have with her, though you haven't mentioned it—in order to do what you've already had her do? What else could be done with that object? What odd character trait does she already have that might make her do something decisive next? What confusion do we already know about, and what mistake could it lead to? What relevant skill will a person have if we already know she works in an antiques shop or raises goats? And where are these people, anyway? In what city, what region or country? Some new writers are reluctant to allow place into their work, but (paradoxically) stories become more universal, not less, when they are more specific—when the people are doing what people do in northern Michigan or central Florida or Springfield, Massachusetts. What goes on there that could change the story? If it's Chicago, did the subway train just get crowded with people leaving Wrigley Field, making conversation difficult? If it's Cape Cod, is someone allergic to shellfish? Susceptible to sunburn? More at ease in a boat than someone else?

If nothing works, sit and do nothing. Suffer for a while. We've considered the need to waste time—waste some. Listen. Imagination will eventually present a situation or give you a person or a place—something, something to start with, which you can gradually add to, making what will, like the spider's web, stretch from one point to another, on which you can hang in the air.

CHAPTER 3

What to Do with a Good Idea

Thoughts Jotted Down

Not long ago I had dinner with my cousin Arnie and his wife, Margaret. He's a doctor; she's a psychologist. They have formidable talents and areas of expertise, but they don't write fiction, and one of the many reasons I enjoy them is that they think it's cool that I do. Arnie used to send me descriptions of fiction he disliked—or actual pieces of bad fiction—asking me, the authority, to tell him if they were as bad as he thought. They always were, and after a while I told him I wouldn't read any more bad fiction and he should stop sending it.

At dinner Arnie related an anecdote a friend had told him and Margaret: when the friend and her husband had houseguests, the visit was spoiled, despite great plans, by a series of minor catastrophes—rain, noisy construction next door, a broken toilet. It was one of those mildly amusing bad-luck stories in which the pleasure comes from yet another addition to the pileup of disasters. All well and good. But then, Arnie explained, his friend decided she would *write a short story* consisting of the funny story she had told them—and the result was not funny, he said, and not really a short story at all. He had not sent it to me, remembering my rule. But he wanted to know: What was it, if it wasn't a short story? Why did he like the story when his friend told it over dinner and dislike it on paper? What might make it a real short story?

If you've ever been in a fiction workshop, you'll know what I said: the anecdote was a *vignette*, an incident, not quite a story. The spoken story worked because nothing more was required than amusement, but the written story didn't because not enough, as we say, was at stake. I suppose readers might enjoy a funny story in which not much is at stake, but the account of disasters would be wilder and funnier. And in extremely funny stories, though not much may actually be at stake, in the circumstances it feels as if lots is at stake; an improbable but logical process convinces us (for the moment) that the characters simply *must* succeed at some outlandish scheme. But it didn't sound as if Arnie's friend was interested in creating farce. The story she wrote would have to become more serious. I suggested that maybe this narrative would work as a short story if the protagonists—the hosts—were not getting along . . . and the husband was a painter . . . and the wife got more and more irritated by the unimportant catastrophes . . . until she blurted out, "I've never liked your paintings!" Thus, minor catastrophes could spoil a marriage. I was rather pleased with this burst of invention, and Arnie and Margaret were impressed.

What if Arnie's friend wanted to improve her written account of the bad visit *without* inventing? What if she wanted to write memoir, not fiction? The piece would still need something at stake, something to keep a reader involved. She might use her imagination not to invent but to remember—to find in her own history something to give this incident substance and meaning. Maybe she'd ask herself why she cared so much about the bad visit, what continued to bug her about it. Possibly there was a time—in her childhood, or

when she was first married, or in her parents' old age: a time of
vulnerability—when minor catastrophes *did* lead to a major catastrophe, when trivial problems changed something important for
the worse. She'd have to be open to trouble, of course: she couldn't
write the story well if she couldn't bear to remember and relive
trouble. The burst of imagination here, the leap, would be not a leap
of invention but a leap of memory.

In both instances—the fictional approach and the nonfictional
approach—the story's structure would change. There would be
something more at the end: as Arnie told the story, it didn't have
an ending. But in order to make the ending matter, the writer
would probably have to go back and change the beginning, or
change things along the way—a few references to those paintings,
or to the childhood memory—so the ending, when it came, would
be powerful. Arnie had noticed that the writer of the story hadn't
yet done something to the material she began with—the factual
incident—to turn it into a made thing.

How do any of us proceed from the bits of ideas we jot down—
in a notebook or a computer file or on a paper napkin? How do we
get from A (which is whatever we start with, whether it's something that came to mind through an imaginative exercise like
those in Chapter 2, or something overheard or glimpsed, a sound,
a memory, an incident someone tells us about, or the feeling that
what we write will have a pillow in it, or the color orange) to B to
C to D? This question applies to all imaginative writing. Fiction
writers sometimes think that memoirists have it easy because the
thing actually happened, but those who write memoir also start
with almost nothing. They have a scrap of an idea that probably
couldn't be written about—surely it would be pointless and shapeless, and everyone would hate it. And then they see a context, a place
to start, and what might come next. Where did these realizations

come from? How do any writers proceed from a fragmentary thought to something finished?

What Almost Happened, What Could Have Happened

Let's slow down. There's no better way to learn to write than to watch other authors—surreptitiously, if possible—and maybe pick up a few tricks, see how they solved the problems we're facing. A finished book tries to keep its secrets. Knocked flat by the author's skill, we aren't supposed to ask how she organized that scene. We can't know how writers come up with stories (often, even in retrospect, how we ourselves did it), but now and then a writer leaves tracks we can follow: we almost catch sight of him or her moving along. Periodically, in this book, we'll stop to look at somebody's work.

William Maxwell, who lived from 1908 to 2000, wrote stories and novels set sometimes in Illinois, where he lived as a child, and sometimes in New York, where he had a long career as a *New Yorker* editor. He used autobiographical material to write fiction—used it imaginatively, in quite different ways at different times.

The enormous fact in Maxwell's life—which apparently demanded to appear in his stories again and again—was that his mother died when he was ten years old, in the flu epidemic of 1918 and 1919. In three of his novels—*They Came Like Swallows, The Folded Leaf,* and *So Long, See You Tomorrow*—the beloved mother of a young, sensitive boy dies of the flu, and Maxwell also told the story in his nonfiction account of his family, *Ancestors*.

They Came Like Swallows, an early novel published in 1937, gives us the experience of an eight-year-old boy, then his older brother, and finally his father. The narrative grows more mature and less subjective as the book progresses, moving from the consciousness of a young child, to an older child's mind, to an adult's. In the first section we follow the moment-by-moment perceptions and thoughts of Bunny, the little boy, as he dozes on a sofa while his mother and aunt talk.

> Bunny's eyelashes brushed and became momen-
> tarily entangled. Against the light from the bay window
> they seemed as large and long as spears. His mother got
> up and went over to the mantel. Then she came back
> and sat down again, with a box on her knee.

He learns that his mother is having a baby—he does not approve—and he tries to explain to her that a classmate has come down with the flu. He too becomes sick, as bells ring because the war has ended in Europe.

In the older brother's section, we learn that the doctor has told the pregnant mother to stay out of the sick boy's room, but when a bird gets into the room, they all forget, and the older brother, his mother, and his aunt chase the bird out. A few weeks later the parents travel to a larger city, where the baby is born in a hospital, and both parents also come down with the flu. This section ends with the older brother's realization, as he lies in bed listening to his relatives talk, that his mother has died. He blames himself for letting her run into Bunny's room when they chased the bird.

In the last part of the novel, the father, who also blames himself for the mother's death, gradually finds the will to go on with his life and take care of his children. Someone convinces the older brother that his mother didn't catch the flu from Bunny. The father comes to think, "And anyway, it was what people intended to do that counted—not what came about because of anything they did."

He and the older brother pace through the house, his arm on the boy's shoulder, and without intending it, they arrive at the mother's coffin, then turn away—to lead their lives somehow.

Nothing in Maxwell's nonfiction suggests that this is exactly what happened in real life. He wrote factually about his mother's death in two books: *Ancestors* is nonfiction, a history of his family published in 1971; and *So Long, See You Tomorrow*, a novel, tells what seems to be the truth. Maxwell was ten when his mother died, but Bunny is eight, less aware yet more imaginatively free than a ten-year-old would be. In the factual stories, it is Maxwell himself, not his older brother, who paces with his father. In *They Came Like Swallows* it must be the brother, since he and the father are the ones who pass through guilt and despair to a partial resolution. Maxwell wrote the book he wanted to write, or could write, at that time.

At the end of *So Long, See You Tomorrow*, Maxwell writes of his mother's death, "Other children could have borne it, have borne it. My older brother did, somehow. *I* couldn't." Nothing in *They Came Like Swallows* denies this truth, but it isn't expressed there—the book is not about whether Bunny can bear it (though we can guess) but about whether his father and brother can.

Another novel, *The Chateau* (1961), about a couple who visit France in the 1950s, is *not* about a mother's death, yet it includes a few pages about the boyhood of the man Maxwell calls Harold Rhodes, listing the many people who make up his adult self. One is "the child his mother went in to cover on her rounds, the last thing at night before she went to bed," and another is "the child of seven . . . who is being taken, with his hand in his father's much bigger hand, to see his mother in the hospital on a day that, as it turned out, she was much too sick to see anyone." Maxwell changes facts even in such brief references: the boy is seven; he tries to visit his mother in the hospital, his hand in his father's. In reality, as

Maxwell relates in *Ancestors* as well as in *They Came Like Swallows*, the father was sick in the same hospital, and the children were at a distance, but if the mother's death is to have only one line, it needs a visual image.

In *The Folded Leaf* (1945), the boy is ten when his mother dies. It begins when Lymie Peters is a high school student and ends when he is almost through college. The book is mostly about a friendship between Lymie—who is thin, sensitive, terrible at games, a good student—and Spud Latham, who is strong and athletic. Lymie has no family to speak of: he is an only child, and his father is a shiftless drinker who stays out late, unlike Maxwell's real father, a respectable businessman. Lymie loves Spud without question and puts up with his friend's shifts from indifference to annoyance to friendliness. When Spud rejects him, Lymie attempts suicide. This novel can be read as a book about unconscious homosexual love, but the point about Lymie's love for Spud is not that Spud is a man but that Lymie is helpless. His passivity would be incomprehensible if we didn't know that Lymie lost his mother and lived through that lonely adolescence.

I don't know whether William Maxwell had a friend like Spud, but he didn't live in Lymie's isolation: he had two brothers; his father remarried. In both this book and *So Long, See You Tomorrow*, the boy dislikes his father's drinking parties, but in the latter, the parties are just parties—embarrassing occasions of letting loose during an otherwise disciplined life—not evidence of a father's failure. If Maxwell did experience some of what's in *The Folded Leaf*, he did so not as Lymie Peters but as William Maxwell. The choice of subject matter—Lymie's vulnerability—dictates the choice of incident and plot.

Many years passed before William Maxwell wrote *So Long, See You Tomorrow*, which came out in 1980, when he was over seventy.

Again, he told the story of his mother's death, but this time, judging from what he wrote in *Ancestors*, he tells plain facts. And, indeed, he tells them as one might tell a true story from memory: it's summarized rather than dramatized, with no dialogue.

When Maxwell was a teenager, his father remarried and had a house built for his new family, and in *So Long, See You Tomorrow*, the narrator recalls going to the unfinished house after the workmen had left it, day after day, and playing there with a boy he knew slightly. Several years later he glimpsed that boy elsewhere but didn't greet him. The boy's father had killed someone, and the narrator—or Maxwell; parts of this novel appear to be memoir—writes that he had long regretted not speaking to the boy.

Maxwell recounts the facts of the crime from historical sources, and then, as a kind of recompense to the boy, tells the imagined, detailed, psychologically subtle story of a tenant farmer who falls in love with his friend's wife and is killed by him. This part of the book is written from the viewpoint of each of the characters in turn—the two men, their wives, and even, famously, the dog. All are deluded; all are lovable.

It's dizzying to see how boldly and freely Maxwell combines the real and the imagined. When telling the facts makes sense for a particular book, he tells the facts. When there aren't enough facts to give us a rich, full story, he invents—moves straight into a fully imagined story, yet one that suits the facts, that doesn't make the facts implausible. When a fact is almost but not quite right for a book, he changes it just a little. Like any good writer, Maxwell knows how to create a moment that feels real though it isn't. What's more to the point is that he makes those moments into coherent stories, by finding details or inventing details that will give point to the struggles of one character or another. In some of his books, he does this by creating scenes around facts that he doesn't alter; in others, by altering facts until the narrative says what he needs it to say, then creating scenes around these new facts. He lets himself imagine.

Facts Denied

Alfred and Emily, by Doris Lessing, is an old person's book, published in 2008, when Lessing was eighty-nine. Like Maxwell's books, it tells the same story more than once, differently. It too may give us some insight into how an author may move beyond whatever she starts with. Lessing explains in a foreword that the book is about her parents and that "the First World War did them both in." And so she has written an account of her parents' lives as they might have been if the war had never taken place: it's the first half of the book. The second half is memoir—what really happened. Many authors write a story or poem or essay to rescue their parents from their mistakes and hardships, but I don't know of another book that does it this way.

The first half of the book, which Lessing calls a novella, summarizes Alfred Tayler and Emily McVeagh's entire lives (their imaginary lives). To feel completely the poignance and power of the novella, one must read the part of the book that comes second, the memoir. There, never deviating from what she can remember, Lessing tells her parents' real story. Her mother became a nurse and was emotionally destroyed by nursing wounded soldiers. Her father wanted to be an English farmer, but lost his leg in the war. When they were married, they left England to live in what was then called Rhodesia, where he bought a barren, lonely farm. Believing in colonialism, they expected the lively social life of a British colony, where they'd live among other Europeans, whose art, literature, and culture would civilize the natives. Her mother brought evening gowns, which moths ate.

The farm failed, and her father died. The mother told stories and ordered English books for her daughter—and that seems to be one of Doris Lessing's few happy memories of her. On the whole, mother and daughter did not get along. The dominant emotion here is rage. "Do children feel their parents' emotions?" Lessing asks. "Yes, we do, and it is a legacy I could have done without."

In the first, imaginary half of the book—not a deviation from the truth but the sort of new truth that arises when one important fact is altered, as in much science fiction (which Lessing also wrote)—Alfred and Emily are friends but don't marry. After a difficult childhood, Alfred is taken into a friend's family and works on their farm. The friend drinks, but Alfred and the woman he marries keep an eye on him, and he eventually gives up drinking and marries. They all raise children on the farm, Alfred playing the role of the prudent elder brother. As decades pass and England has not been in a war, the young people romanticize wars in other countries and run off to join foreign armies. Aside from that, all is well with Alfred, and he lives to be old.

Emily becomes a nurse against her father's wishes, as she did in real life, then gives it up to marry a handsome, rich doctor. It's a childless, sexually unsatisfying marriage in which she runs his fancy house. He dies young, and Emily doesn't know what to do with the rest of her life.

A woman named Mary Lane befriended both Alfred and Emily when they were young, and now Emily goes to stay with Mary in the country. There, by chance, she is left alone with a child for several hours, and finds herself telling stories. It turns out she's good at it, and more and more, she tells stories and people listen.

Mary asks, "Where do you get all these ideas from?" and Emily says, "I don't know."

Her narrative gift determines her life: with friends, she uses her husband's money and raises more, so as to order books and open Montessori schools all over England. She becomes a powerful, energetic head of a complicated charity. There is trouble, but it is resolved. She loves someone. Emily dies at seventy-three, the age at which Lessing's real mother died.

There is little or no plot. Since her parents don't marry, there is no child to correspond to Doris Lessing, and without the war, there's no conflict or source of trouble. If the war did her parents in, it also created the lives they lived. Without war, we read about a pastoral landscape. The lives of shepherds in pastoral literature are not depicted realistically, and pastoral literature doesn't have the swift forward movement of conventional fiction: what shapes such literature is absence. In pastorals of past centuries, what's absent is often the city; the country (unrealistically) is cleaner, safer, more innocent. Here, what's missing is the true, brutal history everyone has to deal with. Without it, Albert and Emily's lives are admirable but vacant; in real life, history supplies tension and direction.

The novella is sorrowful, even though it's the happy version of her parents' lives. Lessing gives a few hints of the origin of particular events or characters—photographs, chance remarks that led her to know what choices her parents might have made. But sorrow and anger are the real source of the alterations Lessing makes to real life.

Story as a Figure of Speech

A useful way to understand what we do, usually unconsciously, when we develop our ideas into stories, may be to think about figures of speech: metaphor, simile, personification, hyperbole. We cannot bear to write down the truth—or writing down the truth will not say enough—so we find another way, either by looking for something that resembles what we cannot put down on paper, or by describing something by means of something else. I'm not talking about using figures of speech to create a more elaborate style. Though they can make memorable and thrilling moments in literature, often they're unnecessary—the facts are enough if you have the right facts—and sometimes imagery obscures feeling instead of clarifying it. I'm talking about using figures of speech to write about what we cannot otherwise bear to write about.

A story itself—a whole long novel—may be a metaphor: the events in the story don't *resemble* what happened in real life, but *stand for* what happened. Someone may write a story about a death, for instance, to express feelings of loss about something intangible.

Hyperbole is exaggeration. A writer who fears disapproval may have a fantasy—or write a story—about being the victim of violence. Someone who delays something important for months may write a story about a character who delays something important for decades.

A story may become possible to write because of personification. A writer gives body and personality to what began as an abstract idea or fear; your nagging doubts become a skeptical relative who always expects failure.

Litotes is the name for a figure of speech in which something is stated by denying its opposite, like saying "not bad" for "good." Lessing's novella can be seen as a lengthy litotes, and the point and power of it are in what is omitted, denied: the war and everything that followed.

Synecdoche is an exact description of one or two actions or objects, as a way of conveying the feel of a situation—using a part of something to evoke the whole. The telling detail can be an emblem of the whole, as when Maxwell specifies that the boy about to lose his mother has his hand in his father's.

We should think of figures of speech not as artifice but as vehicles for more than we can say. Like dreams, they embody what otherwise can't be taken in because it's too vague, too embarrassing, or too dreadful.

In Lessing's book, Mary Lane asks Emily where she gets her ideas, and Emily doesn't know. When they come, stories seem to come from nowhere. But *we* know something about the origin of Emily's stories. She begins telling a story to a child by personifying the cat and mice in the pantry, but what matters is *when* she does that: when she goes to the country, to the sheltered place where she grew up, and faces the losses in her life.

Once we're comfortable with the way the imagination works, we may allow ourselves to dream up stories that originate in a figurative version of the real world. Years after your divorce is final, you may realize that your novel about soldiers at war was a metaphor for your private conflict; or your story about an arsonist who gleefully burns down a house was your expression of rage at an obnoxious neighbor, though all you did in real life was write a polite note. Probably your book is better for your ignorance of what you were doing. Planning this sort of thing makes the results feel forced and phony.

From Theme to Story

Mark Twain tried three times to write his last novel, *The Mysterious Stranger*, but never finished it. If you read this book before 1969, you read a version published in 1916, six years after the author's death, by his biographer and literary executor Albert Bigelow Paine. Samuel Clemens was unhappy and deluded at the end of his life: depressed, cynical, paranoid, and infatuated with a series of preteen girls, whom he called "the angelfish." Some people around him did their best to obscure the great author's last years, and that may be why Paine, when he came to publish what he called *The Mysterious Stranger, A Romance*, chose to print the unfinished first of the three versions, which Twain had called *The Chronicle of Young Satan*. Paine ended it with the last chapter of the last version, writing what he needed for a coherent narrative and making many other changes.

It wasn't until 1969 that William Gibson edited the complete set of original manuscripts, and since then, if you buy a copy of what's called *No. 44, The Mysterious Stranger*, you're buying the last version. This shocking textual history and the way it's been interpreted— Bernard DeVoto wrote that with the version Paine published, Mark Twain "came back from the edge of insanity, and found as much peace as any man may find in his last years"—make it hard to look at the three versions simply as three drafts by a writer of fiction who tried to turn his initial idea into a story. Nonetheless, let's see what we can learn if we examine it that way.

Like Maxwell and Lessing, Twain began with intense feeling, but unlike those writers, he didn't invent around or in contrast to real events. He began with an abstract idea and devised a story that illustrated it. In his introduction to *The Mysterious Stranger Manuscripts*, Gibson quotes from one of Twain's notebooks, written in 1895, two years before he began this book.

It is the strangest thing, that the world is not full of books that scoff at the pitiful world, and the useless universe and the vile and contemptible human race— books that laugh at the whole paltry scheme and deride it. . . . Why don't *I* write such a book? Because I have a family. There is no other reason.

The first version, *The Chronicle of Young Satan*, takes place in a village in Austria in 1702. An attractive young man appears to three boys and tells them he is an angel and his name is Satan—he is a nephew of the Satan we know about. When the boys want to smoke but have no source of fire, he blows on their tobacco and ignites it: he can do tricks. He makes a village of clay in which people and animals come to life, and the boys watch in delight. But when Satan grows tired of the village, he destroys it, and the tiny creatures scream in pain and fear. As the story proceeds, the young man continues to perform impressive supernatural acts and to argue that moral feeling causes nothing but trouble. He tells two of the boys that the third will drown, and sure enough, they are unable to prevent his death. Aside from some plot about a wrongly accused priest, the story consists entirely of Satan rejecting morality and doing tricks: all the incidents arise from the idea. Twain, this time, moved perhaps too consciously from his theme to an embodiment of it. The story is predictable and breaks off without concluding.

The second version Twain wrote, *Schoolhouse Hill*, is much shorter. It takes place in an American town like the one where Samuel Clemens grew up, at the time of his boyhood. The children getting out of school when a mysterious youth appears include Tom Sawyer, Becky Thatcher, and Huck Finn. Here the attractive stranger, who again performs wonders, is called 44. Mark Twain brings in 44's lack of a moral sense more gradually, and there are more characters and richer characters than in the first version. This stranger doesn't just do tricks. But there's no story; everything here, still, arises directly from the idea the author wanted to demonstrate.

Mark Twain was a great writer, but everybody has to start somewhere with each new project, and he was old and tired. What he wrote is something like what the rest of us may come up with when we know the theme of a story before anything else. It's tempting to make every incident demonstrate the theme, and to expound the theme immediately. It's not until we put theme aside temporarily that the story can make a thematic point without preaching.

In the third version, *No. 44, The Mysterious Stranger*, Twain temporarily turns away from theme. We're in an Austrian village again, but this time it's 1490, shortly after the invention of the printing press. Printing, in this version, is the subject that Mark Twain needed. Printing itself doesn't demonstrate the vileness of humanity or the cruelty of people who think they are moral. But it suggests characters and events: a story. An author needs situations in the real world, tangible problems and enterprises, or else the characters can do little more than argue about the theme. Unhappy people who just sit in their living room can only exchange insults—"You're stingy"; "You're careless"—but if you set your story in an amusement park, they can disagree about what to do when the ice-cream vendor cheats them or the Ferris wheel breaks down while they're on it. Twain's third version is still about selfishness and cruelty, but now it plays out in real events.

The narrator, August, is an apprentice in a print shop belonging to a man who owns and lives in a castle with his family, servants, and pets, in addition to a crew of printers. Finally there are enough characters and relationships—maybe even too many. Yet again a mysterious but attractive young man called 44 appears, this time in want of work. Again he can perform tricks—make food appear, and so on. August helps 44 learn the printing trade. Plot complexities abound, some funny and interesting, some labored. The trickster turns a snobbish maid into a cat. He completes a print job

when some of the crew go on strike. He creates clones of the printers, and when one is found where he isn't supposed to be, the original printer is blamed. Mark Twain makes his point—the moral
sense is the source of trouble—but he makes it while much else
goes on as well. Some of 44's tricks are tiresome, but some are
funny.

This version contains realistic details about printing, as well as
lively dialogue, interesting characters, and a bit of a plot. At the
end—this one comes to a conclusion—August and 44 part. When 44
leaves, saying they'll never meet again, August says, "In this life,
44, but in another? We shall meet in another, surely, 44?" To which
44 replies, *There is no other.* When August doubts him, 44 says,
"There is no God, no universe, no human race, no earthly life, no
heaven, no hell."

The book ends with August's declaration, "He vanished, and
left me appalled; for I knew, and realized, that all he had said was
true."

So how did Mark Twain get from A to B? By starting with intense
feeling and groping toward story, I suppose, as the rest of us do.
He began with his despair, his idea—which obviously shocked
him—that the universe isn't moral, that there is no other life, no
meaning. He found a character, the mysterious stranger, who in
each of the versions is charming, powerful, and amoral. Then he
needed a story. And it took him three tries to find one. Not bad. As
soon as he thought, "Print shop," he seems to have arrived easily—
the writing becomes fast-paced and lively—at his castle and its
inhabitants. Bringing in 44's capacities leads to complication piled
upon complication. By the end, theme dominates again, and the
last scenes are little more than demonstrations of it. It's not Mark

Twain's best book, but 44 is dazzling and the narrator, August, appealing. The theme is more convincingly dark than in the earlier versions, and maybe that's why Twain's posthumous editor suppressed this final draft.

What we call the making of story—whether for fiction, personal essay, or poetry—is usually the act of elaborating: writing down an incident where before there was a general truth (or an idea or image or fact), or writing a series of incidents where before, in imagination or memory, there was just one. Any moment—whether it is imaginary or not—is only one of a great number of moments that *could* be written about. To use one's imagination is to resist assuming that only one thing can happen in a piece of writing: the one that happened in life, or the one we already thought of.

The writer whose imagination moves freely will also see various ways to use what she began with—as Maxwell began with the death of his mother and altered the story to suit various purposes, as Lessing began with her parents' stark lives and imagined their development from a different starting point. We must open our minds so as to be flexible enough to see how to write the next project. And we need to be open to the intense feelings, whatever they may be, that have made it necessary and possible for us to write it. Openness to the strength of our own feelings will make us able to choose topics or incidents weighty enough to correspond to the size of our emotions, and if they matter that much to us, they will make a difference to readers. Then we'll need to shape our pieces of writing, of course; to revise three times or three hundred times—to yank the string. But first the kite must fly.

We get our ideas, then, by listening for them, but listening with enough patience and playfulness, enough attention to what we're listening for, that what we hear won't overwhelm or frighten us. We have to listen to ourselves like psychotherapists who have learned not to be shocked at what people come up with or at the intensity of their need. We start with highly charged thoughts: abstract ideas or memories of our lives or images or colors or incidents we've heard of or imagined. And then we get more ideas by being willing to receive them. Intensity takes us to the next step by means of imaginative transformation: changing the general to the particular or the abstract to the concrete, giving an example, bringing an idea to life as a person, imagining something as something else it resembles, or considering time: what happened next, what *could* happen next? And then we need to write down what comes to mind before we lose our nerve.

CHAPTER 4

Let Happenings Happen

Make Trouble

I was recently waiting in the checkout line at the Italian market in my neighborhood, where a recording of Luciano Pavarotti sings at you while you're choosing vegetables, and conversation is often in Italian, when a man behind me asked the cashier, "Did you go to the christening party?"

"Yes."

"Was there any drama?"

"No."

"I guess that's . . . good," he said.

Maybe it was good for the christening party (maybe not), but it's not so good for the *story* of the christening party if there was no drama.

Sometimes, in fiction by new writers, nothing happens for reasons that don't have to do with the effort of thinking up events. I've realized that many writers—even if their work is not autobiographical—don't *want* to write about events, or even believe they shouldn't. Although the kite is starting to fly, the restraining string in this instance isn't common sense, but something more like panic, which pulls the kite down to the ground.

Much in the writing business, as we've noticed, requires a certain amount of nerve, if not outright courage: it isn't enough to sit down at the computer, confront the blank page, and type words, though heaven knows that can be hard enough. Having the will to use what a writer has learned may be harder than learning it, harder than making the decision to write in the first place. For some people, it feels safer and more pleasant to write stories in which nothing happens, or nothing but feeling—people feeling bad, feeling slightly better, feeling slightly worse.

Without trouble, though, there's no story. There must be drama at the christening party. Little Red Riding Hood must meet the wolf. I know people who are tempted to make the story be about Little Red's mixed feelings about her grandmother, who fails to understand her granddaughter and has terrible politics. In life, the granddaughter's feelings are interesting enough—and maybe one unforgettable day she will blurt them out. But if a story is to be worth reading by someone other than Little Red herself, the burst of feeling probably should be embodied in an action that might change things, even if ultimately it doesn't. The wolf makes anger and hatred tangible. We need the capacity of the wolf to do something large—to eat Grandmother—whether this is the version of the story in which that's exactly what happens or the version in which Grandmother is saved. That is: you don't necessarily need life-changing action—but you need, at least, the plausible threat of life-changing action that's then prevented.

Why do writers avoid that? Sometimes for the reasons I had, back when I was learning to write: I liked fiction's capacity to depict thought and feeling so much that I figured the more thought and feeling, the better, and why bother with anything else? I confused the question of what makes an interesting moment in a narrative with what makes it a story. Similarly, students I've taught sometimes want more than anything else to write about passivity—about people who *can't* take action—and so the authors emphatically want *nothing* to happen in their stories. You can write good stories about anyone you care to write about, though I confess to a certain sinking of the heart when my new student tells me that passive people are those she likes to write about most. And of course the category of passive people includes the interesting subcategory of passive women obsessed with bad men—many volumes of fiction are all about them. If this kind of subject matter attracts you, it may be worthwhile to reread some of your favorite authors carefully, noting what makes the story move along, whether the character moves or not. There must be something—action by someone else, or maybe what are sometimes called acts of God: storms, floods, fires—that starts up suspense in the reader, that makes us wonder what will happen. Or there's action that *might* take place and doesn't. Just as the delight of the inner life rarely provides entire stories, similarly, the miseries of passivity don't make entire stories either. Don't confuse the nature of the characters with the structure that tells us about them.

Another reason for resisting action, I suspect, is that some people (surely not *you*) believe that inventing and writing about bad things makes them likelier to happen. If anyone you know has this problem, it will help if that person creates characters who are distinctly fictional, and are not based on the writer or the writer's family and friends. I too wouldn't want to make a character get hurt, robbed, betrayed, abandoned, or cheated—or to make that character hurt, rob, betray, abandon, or cheat others—if I was picturing my sister. And I don't think my friends and family would appreciate recognizing themselves in a story in which they then die of cancer or rob somebody at gunpoint. So this is yet another reason to invent rather than basing fiction on life.

Making up bad events doesn't cause them to happen—but it can recall them to mind. If the piece is memoir, or—assuming it's fiction—if the bad event is based on something in the writer's life, some lapse in the writer, some loss, some terrible experience, it takes nerve to endure the pain of reliving it. Even if a story is entirely invented, the characters' emotions will inevitably be ones the writer has felt. It's understandable that you'd rather not put yourself through fear or jealousy or anger again—but maybe your story requires that you do so whether you like doing it or not.

Furthermore, it's hard to inflict pain on one's characters, even if they are imaginary. A shrewd student, after noting all the obstacles faced by the main character in an elaborately plotted novel she read, commented that fiction writers need "sadistic ingenuity." It takes a certain pleasure in inflicting pain to put a fictional character through enough trouble for a story, let alone a novel. Most of us don't like being sadistic, even toward imaginary people. I don't mind giving my characters obstacles and problems, but the first time I killed somebody, though he was old, imaginary, and dead of natural causes, I burst into tears.

A writer I worked with recently kept sending me drafts—which were good to start with and better each time I saw them—of the opening chapters of a novel about a woman trying to get her life going after a bad stretch. Every draft, in more or less detail, included the same episode from when the character was a teenager: on a whim, she committed a series of minor but interestingly subversive acts of vandalism. Suddenly, maybe the fourth time I read this material (which the writer kept reorganizing), the girl committed her crime only once. Someone else caused the rest of the trouble.

I knew this character well and had watched her emerge through drafts that revealed her more and more clearly and meaningfully. When her mischief-making nearly disappeared, I felt cheated, as if I'd gone to a performance of *Hamlet* in which the prince only nicked Polonius through the arras.

It was instructive to learn why my student had changed the story. She admitted that she liked her character—so she was "coddling" her. The more she had thought about what she'd written, the clearer it became that committing this crime would make a difference in the girl's life. Maybe she wouldn't be able to go to college. My student (who quickly saw the flaw in her thinking; I'm telling you this not because this student is incompetent but because she's first-rate, and if she fell into this error, anyone might) hadn't wanted to put her character through something so bad.

Characters aren't interesting and fully real until they do wrong and have problems. Think how boring it is to hear, "And my nephew got into a top law school and met a wonderful girl. . . ." It's in our bad behavior and misfortune that we become worth hearing about, alas. The reader will like my student's character more, not less, when she does something naughty, daring, and zany. We shouldn't shelter our characters and prevent them from living full lives, surely, any more than we want to deprive our children of experience, though we feel even worse when kids we love suffer.

It's not enough to give characters trouble. As my student foresaw, if she told the story realistically, her girl's bad behavior would lead to unpleasant consequences. In life it's usually good to solve problems quickly. If you and a friend have a misunderstanding, the sooner you clear it up, the better. But numerous stories, novels, and films depend for subject matter on misunderstandings that don't just persist, but worsen. In life, accidents should be avoided, and when they happen, it's best to act quickly and prevent further mishaps. But in a story, trouble is good and complications are even better—as long as they exist not just to make things upsetting but to give characters a chance to make mistakes or solve problems, bring out latent desires and fears and needs, precipitate the next event. In a story, if a jar of honey shatters on the floor just as the baby crawls in that direction, you need to stifle your impulse to snatch up the baby. We don't want the baby to cut her fingers just so we can hurt the poor baby—I'm not advocating sadism for its own sake. But if the baby's injury causes her parents to fire the apparently neglectful babysitter, leading to strain in their marriage as they try to manage without her, or causing the sitter—now jobless—to let her former boyfriend persuade her to become a drug courier after all, then maybe the doorbell must ring as the jar falls, so the babysitter, distracted, doesn't grab the baby. Resist the temptation to solve your characters' problems for them. On the contrary, when a problem comes up, think what more you can do with it. Problems lead to story.

Don't Be Melodramatic—but Be Dramatic

Here's another reason my students don't want the baby to get cut on the broken glass: it will be "melodramatic." I can't count the number of times students have told me they considered having some much-needed significant event occur in their fiction, but didn't, to avoid being melodramatic. "Melodrama," as the word itself suggests, originally referred to a play with music, or to a section of a play or opera in which a character spoke while music played. Our current sense of melodrama as something to avoid originates with Victorian melodramas—popular plays with exaggerated, one-dimensional characters (villains, heroes, distressed young women) and dreadful catastrophes conveniently averted. Silent films, with their great capacity to show action and exaggerated personality traits, and their lack of subtle conversation, made perfect melodramatic crowd-pleasers.

The difference between melodrama and serious drama or film is not in the *nature* of the events; it's in the quantity and plausibility of the events, and in the language. After I assigned *King Lear* to a class I once taught of adults returning to school, a student burst out, "This is a soap opera!" *King Lear* is different from a soap opera in that most of the characters have ambivalence, complex awareness, and the capacity to change. The language depicts what's going on in ways that speak to universal experience. While the story has plenty of action, there's not so much event that it becomes silly. But, yes, the terrible troubles in *King Lear* might happen in a soap opera. The play greatly moved my nearly illiterate aunt Sarah—who'd been raised on melodramatic Yiddish theater—when the ladies from the senior center went to see Morris Carnovsky, also raised on Yiddish theater, play the king.

Melodrama is exaggerated drama, not simply drama. Don't be melodramatic, but be dramatic, and if you find that what you've written is sentimental, unlikely, or exaggerated beyond plausibility, you can probably fix it by fixing the language you use to tell it. The action itself, if it seems right in your imagination and can plausibly happen in the circumstances you've described, won't feel melodramatic. If it docs, take another look at those circumstances. Have you established earlier that the person who performs the action has it in her to do something like this? Are you describing correctly the objects used in this action? What sort of paperweight could cause an injury like that, and when did the person who threw it pick it up, and how come we didn't know until now that there was a desk in the room, much less a paperweight on it? If there's a gun, what kind? If there's a car, what kind of car, and what's the stretch of road like where the accident happened? Have you added pounding hearts or roiling stomachs to convince your reader that it would be upsetting if a red Ford pickup knocked a white-haired man in a tan Windbreaker off his old Raleigh bicycle, or are you trusting to understatement, letting the facts do the work? If your description of the event isn't effective yet, add a couple more facts, not a description of the onlooker's feelings.

Nearly all the writers I meet—I suspect nearly all the writers reading this book—are trying to write literary fiction, which I would define as any fiction that keeps the reader engaged by depicting complex, believable people with complex, believable problems. That is, the reader does not keep reading primarily because the book includes violence, sex, and terrifying possibilities. But that doesn't mean that literary fiction *doesn't* include violence, sex, and terrifying possibilities.

Many years ago a student of mine sat down for a conference and began to cry. When she could speak, she said, "Elizabeth says my work is—*commercial!*" Elizabeth, her classmate, knew how to get to people. I doubt that nowadays—when marketing departments at publishing houses have plenty to say about any book, no matter how literary—a similar remark would do much harm. Even at the time I refrained from saying what I was thinking, which was "In your dreams!"

A fear of being commercial, however, still seems to grip many new writers, even while they fantasize about writing best sellers. When I complained to a friend that my students weren't making anything happen in their stories, she said maybe they were avoiding material that her mother would call "common." It's true that action links great fiction to schlocky fiction, *King Lear* to the Yiddish theater. Also, writing about action invariably involves the unglamorous physical world. To imagine the results of your character's actions, you must think in practical ways, not literary ones. How long is a flight from Dallas to Boston? What are the symptoms of poison ivy? How do you cook cream sauce? (Don't say it's simmering, as a poet I once heard did in a poem. The mistake made everything he said seem unreliable, because if you can cook, you know it would curdle.) You must learn unromantic, unliterary facts. If you don't want your fiction to be cheap and hackneyed, don't use the facts and literary devices you employ in a cheap and hackneyed way.

Let drama happen—but that need not mean hideous catastrophes. A student I worked with recently had been told "nothing happens in your novel" again and again. I can all but hear him muttering, *"All right, all right!"* through clenched teeth. Into his beautifully sensitive book he inserted an accidental death and a fire that destroyed everything. The events were so terrible that, with his great psychological insight, he accurately depicted the characters as stunned, helpless in the face of them. I found myself asking him to come up with slightly less catastrophic catastrophes: events that would force people to react, not events so huge that life as the characters knew it more or less ceased. Disaster can be an interesting start for a book: a catastrophe occurs in the first chapter; now what? But hideous catastrophes two hundred pages into a story destroy what came before. Who cares if the marriage was going to survive, now that the wife is dead? What does it matter how the children responded to their father's neglect, now that the family is homeless and all its possessions have burned up? Look for trouble that will bring out the best or the worst in your people, not simply finish them off.

Don't (Necessarily) Be Afraid of Coincidence

Let's think for a bit about coincidence. Coincidence in *life*, one should note first, is delectable. For instance: my aunt Sarah (the one who liked *King Lear*) made weekly outings to the department stores in downtown Brooklyn. Once, she told my mother and me a long story about what she had bought and returned that week, mentioning that she ran out of money and lacked bus fare home. Then she stopped. "But how did you get home?" my practical mother asked. Aunt Sarah said matter-of-factly, "I found a five-dollar bill on the sidewalk." To her, the coincidence wasn't worth mentioning.

Another example: My two best friends in college and I had grown up in widely separated parts of New York, but one dark night in a lonely downtown Manhattan neighborhood, we discovered that, in different ways, we'd all met a girl there was no reason any of us should know. And a third: When my graduate school roommate passed her doctoral orals, I celebrated by festooning our apartment with crepe paper streamers, which sagged down to the floor before she came home. While I waited for her, the doorbell rang, and there stood a worker from the gas company, who insisted on ducking under the streamers to make an adjustment to our stove that the state required every seven years. He was just emerging from under the streamers near the door when my roommate finally arrived (just as I'd been called to the phone in the hall) and flung open the door to face a man holding a wrench and rising to meet her.

A good coincidence makes me feel as if I've stepped through a barrier into another place, sometimes forbidden, sometimes zany. Aunt Sarah's coincidence, finding five dollars when she was broke, pleases me because of what her nonchalance says about her—apparently she assumed she'd find the money—and because it suggests, light-heartedly, a caring universe. When one of my college friends happened to mention someone we unknowingly had in common in the impersonal city, it was as if we'd strayed into a parallel existence with rules different from ours. Maybe we were already dead. The experience had the quality Freud called uncanny, describing events we fear because they seem to confirm primitive religious notions that civilized people have repressed.

My roommate meeting the man from the gas company was funny, but something more. Something else about my roommate and me: later in life I married a man, and her lifelong partner was a woman. This was decades ago, before gay liberation, and she had sometimes wondered nervously if she might be a lesbian; I hadn't had the courage to pose the question about myself, but in retrospect I know we were attracted to each other. She was uncomfortable in the presence of many men, and that year I had a boyfriend. I was clueless and clumsy, and she was often angry with me, while I thought the problem was hers.

Though the convergence of the crepe paper streamers, the man from the gas company, and my roommate still pleases me simply because it was so unlikely, I am struck now at how the sudden appearance of a man with a wrench might have felt to her—perhaps emblematic of the distress I'd been causing her all year. Two things happened to happen, my roommate's doctoral orals and the arrival of the man (calmly announcing his once-every-seven-years mission like a creature in a fairy tale), and the two things belonged—for serious as well as comic reasons—in the same story.

All this seems valuable for fiction, doesn't it?—all this strangeness and unpredictability. Yet we know that coincidence in fiction, alas, is different. Literature is full of coincidence: everyone connected with the crisis appears at the same place at once; unremarked strangers turn out to be long-lost relatives; unimportant visitors happen to know the secret. Coincidence in fiction makes us feel not that the universe of the story is interestingly unpredictable, but that it's excessively controlled, heavy, and obvious. In real life we don't expect coincidence and are excited by it because it's unlikely but true. If I invent Aunt Sarah and the five dollars, the thrill disappears.

At the end of Dickens's *Great Expectations*, the main character, Pip, by chance meets Estella, the arrogant woman he has loved all his life, at the site of a romantically ruined house at moonrise. Estella tells Pip she was wrong not to care about him, and Pip tells us, "The evening mists were rising now, and in all the broad expanse of tranquil light they showed to me, I saw no shadow of another parting from her." End of book. Dickens had originally written the ending differently, making Pip and Estella spot each other on a city street in circumstances that couldn't lead to anything. Though the revised ending he used (he yielded to pressure) leaves the happy future a bit uncertain, this is the kind of coincidence that gives coincidence a bad name. We can enjoy some coincidences in nineteenth-century fiction only if we bring a set of critical standards to our reading that is unlike those we apply to serious contemporary literature. In my mind and maybe yours, an ending that depends on wild coincidence cheapens a book and makes it silly.

I wonder how Dickens and others got away with it. Maybe his readers expected the plots of novels to be improbable. Maybe they accepted the coincidences for spiritual reasons: if Providence makes a coincidence happen, it's not a lazy device but a thematic statement. Maybe they were better at suspending disbelief than we are, or maybe they were more naïve. I occasionally meet people who don't quite understand that fiction is invented. If you kept forgetting that *Great Expectations* is fiction—if your sense of the difference between fiction and nonfiction was blurry—would you have the same spooky thrill about the final coincidence that you'd have if it happened in real life to a friend of yours? Did Dickens's first readers come upon that passage not just with tolerance and pleased habituation to the form, but with delight?

If you put a coincidence like the one Dickens used into a story you write, you know it will seem amateurish. I rarely see coincidences in student stories. The clumsy use of coincidence (like the melodramatic use of exciting action) has scared some writers away from coincidence altogether. It's a loss. Don't we want to put into fiction something like Aunt Sarah matter-of-factly refusing to be surprised, or my roommate encountering an absurd situation that resonated with something serious in her life? How?

One way to use coincidence and make it work is to have nothing turn on it. Coincidences feel illegitimate when they solve problems. If the story doesn't benefit from the coincidence, it's simply pretty and suggestive. Another way to make a coincidence work is to begin a story with it. Make it the reason there's a story to tell in the first place. A third is to establish that the community in which your story takes place is one in which coincidence is part of the landscape. People in my town, New Haven, Connecticut, revel in coincidence, and we claim it happens here all the time: you know everyone in more than one way. Maybe this is true in all cities of a certain size—small enough that the barista will turn out to be your office mate's daughter; large enough that you'll be surprised.

It also helps to make coincidence unobtrusive. There's a wild coincidence in E. M. Forster's 1910 novel *Howards End* that doesn't seem to bother most readers. Helen Schlegel, one of the two sisters who are the book's main characters, for complicated reasons brings a working-class couple she has befriended to a wedding reception—and it turns out that the woman she brings was once the mistress of the bride's father, Henry Wilcox, whom Helen's sister, Margaret, is engaged to marry.

Margaret is the character through whom we experience all this. The former mistress, Jacky, is drunk, Henry comes forward to try to get rid of her, and Jacky greets him, "If it isn't Hen!" Margaret, who has no idea what Jacky means, apologizes for the awkward interruption. Henry, recognizing Jacky, imagines that Margaret and Helen have devised a plot to expose him. He says, "Are you now satisfied?"—which baffles Margaret even more. Finally, after a painful page, Henry says, "I have the honor to release you from your engagement," and Forster says of Margaret, "Still she could not understand. She knew of life's seamy side as a theory; she could not grasp it as a fact. More words from Jacky were necessary—words unequivocal, undenied." At that point Margaret begins to speak, stops herself, and then finally says to Henry, "So that woman has been your mistress?"

None of the characters know what's going on, and in the confusion, it's unlikely that anybody notices that the author is manipulating all of us, characters and readers. He's distracted us by concentrating on Margaret's psychology. She can't grasp what has happened, not because it's unlikely that the single lower-class person her sister has befriended should be her fiancé's former mistress, but because she doesn't understand life and sex. The *coincidence* isn't important to Margaret.

Another way to make coincidence work is to put the story into a slightly unfamiliar universe, as in farce—a universe where coincidence is part of the joke. Flannery O'Connor's story "A Good Man Is Hard to Find" is not farce, but the blatant (though useful to the story) coincidence in it doesn't bother readers; I've never heard anyone mention it.

A grandmother scares her family with tales of an escaped convict, The Misfit. She, her son, and his wife and children set out on a trip through Georgia, where The Misfit is thought to be hiding. The family has a car accident, and the person who comes along is The Misfit, who kills them all. The grandmother is whiny, sneaky, and selfish, and every bad thing that happens to the family until The Misfit arrives is her fault. When she breaks out with her son's name, "Bailey Boy, Bailey Boy," at the end, we feel love in the story for the first time.

Why does the coincidence work? You might think its success had to do with Flannery O'Connor's religious universe. Just before The Misfit shoots the grandmother, she looks at him closely and says, "Why you're one of my babies." The grandmother has led this family into evil, evil that is her opportunity. In a universe with God in charge of it, even the difficult, opaque God of Flannery O'Connor, a family can be led, for a reason, down the only dirt road in Georgia where an escaped convict lurks. But nothing in the story suggests that the coincidence is connected to its religious message.

One way to make a coincidence feel less clumsy is to have the author acknowledge that what she is describing is improbable. But O'Connor doesn't. There's no disclaimer, no apology, no paragraph saying that sometimes the strangest things happen.

Not only does the coincidence work, but it gives me the same sort of pleasure as coincidences in my life. It delights me. I think the coincidence is O'Connor's way of letting us know we're in a slightly skewed place in which what happens does not exactly follow the rules we're used to.

But the main reason the coincidence works may be that the characters are so stupid that they don't know coincidence is surprising. The grandmother predicts that they will meet The Misfit, and they do, like people hearing a weather forecast and encountering rain. The narrative voice is almost always as stupid as they are. Here is the grandmother in the car.

> She said she thought it was going to be a good day for driving, neither too hot nor too cold, and she cautioned Bailey that the speed limit was fifty-five miles an hour and that the patrolmen hid themselves behind billboards and small clumps of trees and sped out after you before you had a chance to slow down. She pointed out interesting details of the scenery.

Only later comes a different kind of sentence:

> There was a pistol shot from the woods, followed closely by another. Then silence. The old lady's head jerked around. She could hear the wind move through the tree tops like a long satisfied insuck of breath. "Bailey Boy!" she called.

This narrator would be more than smart enough to point out that running into The Misfit was highly unlikely, but this narrator isn't in evidence at that point in the story. So O'Connor's coincidence is something like Forster's. The *characters* aren't aware of it, or wouldn't call it a coincidence. There's so much that the characters don't get, in this story, that the unlikeliness of the coincidence is just something else that's beyond them. Like Aunt Sarah, who didn't know that finding a five-dollar bill was remarkable, they don't know enough about art to notice the coincidence; they think they're just in life. Coincidences happen in life; they are suspect only in art.

I've been arguing for giving your characters actions to perform, insisting that if fiction only explains how people feel—what is going on for them inwardly—it doesn't fully use its capacity to keep a reader engaged. Making interior experience clear, on the other hand, by finding equivalents for it in external events, or finding external events that resonate with feeling, is endlessly interesting, because we can think up endless numbers of situations that embody the struggles of the inner life, and many events feel like embodiments of inner dramas. Even in ordinary life, you know that the day you receive an impossible assignment at work will be the day you come home to discover that the dishwasher has flooded the kitchen floor. Isn't resonance what makes one event worthy of going into a story and another not worthy? Stories that don't work sometimes include long, boring scenes in which people do something like clean a car window. The trouble is not that nothing is happening but that what happens has no connection to strong feeling, to the inner life. Unless, of course, it's a story like Andre Dubus's "The Winter Father," in which a man who doesn't live with his children takes them to dinner, then has a conversation with them in his car, outside his ex-wife's house.

> Next morning when he got into his car, the inside
> of the windshield was iced. He used the small plastic
> scraper from his glove compartment. As he scraped the
> middle and right side, he realized the grey ice curling

and falling from the glass was the frozen breath of his children.

Consider the morality play, in which abstract qualities like good and evil take form as characters. In the fifteenth-century English play *Everyman*, a man is told by a character named Death that he must undertake a journey from which he won't return. All his ordinary friends (Fellowship, Kindred, and so on) refuse to go with him, but he is finally accompanied by Knowledge and Good Dedes. We still write books about journeys because we are interested in inner journeys; we still write books about conflict because we have taken notice of some inner conflict. Once we consider action not as the sign of cheap fiction, but as the way any fiction embodies the life within us, then it's clear that no single kind of action is superior to any other kind. Anger and conflict can be expressed by means of a novel about a war, but also by a novel about a conflict in the workplace or in a family. There is such a thing as the story or novel in which nothing happens, but that's not the same as the story or novel that makes us care intently whether or not a flower will be picked and then shows us a character surreptitiously picking the flower.

But what makes us care whether the flower is picked or not? A beautiful description of the flower won't do it, and a pathetic description of the person who doesn't want it picked won't do it. What will make us care is some other action or conflict that is going on at the same time and coincides with the picking of the flower: that is, some action that belongs by coincidence. Coincidence, *Webster's Third New International Dictionary* says, means "the concurrence of events or circumstances appropriate to one another or having significance in relation to one another but between which there is no apparent causal connection." That could mean my roommate meeting the man from the gas company under the crepe paper streamers, but it could also mean Stephen Dedalus, in James Joyce's *Portrait of the Artist as a Young Man*, breaking his glasses when he is small and defenseless in a harsh place. Appropriateness, that is, can be the damnedest thing ever, or it can simply be suggestive and interesting. Coincidence could mean the concurrence of somebody's inner sorrow with the privations of the Great Depression or with the anxiety and frustration of the war in Vietnam, Iraq, or Afghanistan. It could mean The Misfit in Flannery O'Connor's story meeting the grandmother, a different kind of misfit. Essentially, coincidence is the coming together of two events. Of course, these coincidences can be clumsy and manipulative as well: you'll need to figure out a way to make your ordinary eighteenth-century Bostonian part of history without having Paul Revere's horse step on his foot.

If, as we make up any story, we start with one event and ask ourselves what else might be happening, we risk obvious coincidences and correspondences, but we give ourselves an exciting opportunity: the chance to bring into our stories events that will make them not merely plausible but arresting. "What else might be going on in the life of this character?" is a question that is not hard to answer, and if we are open, as we write, to the strong feeling in our work, the possibilities that come to mind will often turn out to enliven our stories and tell us more than we knew about what's going on in them.

Coincidence is often what gives fiction its chance to mean something. When two things come together, improbably or not, a spark is struck. Making those things happen simultaneously suggests that meaning is just beyond the surface. Many of us are in rebellion against meaningfulness. Randomness is cool and anything else is slightly nauseating, the sort of profound philosophy that can be inscribed on mugs printed with little rainbows, or posted on Facebook. The risk is that the author is seen scrambling around making it happen, caring too much about meaning. Coincidence is risky.

Coincidence is risky, but risk is good, we all know that. When one of my sons was in a writing program in high school, he was *graded* on risk-taking. "Jacob got an A-minus in risk," I told anyone who'd listen. Aren't we looking for guidance in writing that, unlike the directions provided by rules and formulas, will be unsafe? Of course, it's risky—and often admirable—to write openly about true personal hardship and pain. It's also risky to make up story. If the dictates of craft are safe and limiting, the suggestion that we make an event happen, and try to sense what other event might be going on at the same time, is not just risky; it's stimulating. The kite soars; ideas come.

Using coincidence is part of our opportunity to focus on story, on the way story offers meaning and solace and delight. There is loveliness in things happening and then happening some more—and happening simultaneously—whether on a small or a grand scale. Anything we describe—art or music or sex or a heavy rainstorm—is in the story by report, but the story, its coinciding strands, is there itself, something beautiful no matter what's in it. Writing must always be linear, since we read one word at a time, but nothing in life happens all by itself. Coincidence brings simultaneity into your story. Used thoughtfully, it makes the narrative richer and deeper. Look to the right and left of your characters; see what more they can do, what they *must* do, to articulate in action that inner life we love so much. Like dreams, stories make feeling tangible.

CHAPTER 5

Become Someone Else

Am I Allowed to Pretend I'm You?

A writer I know kept referring to a short story he was working on as "the one in which I am a woman." Not the one in which "I write from the point of view of a woman," not even the one in which "I pretend to be a woman." He was, temporarily, a woman. I think that's what it takes.

Understand the term "point of view" literally. You're writing as Brendan, say, and Brendan wants to perform surgery even if it might not help the dying man. Or Brendan thinks his daughters should go to church, though his wife hates religion. Or has whatever opinion made him your protagonist in the first place. It can be easy to forget that Brendan isn't simply the owner of that opinion, that he's also someone with a literal point of view: he's facing the window, so the sun is in his eyes, and he may see a helicopter pass between the buildings outside, or, in a different setting, a cat on a porch. He sees Miranda's face, sees her elegantly curved eyebrows. One eyebrow twitched when she made fun of his pastor. Brendan's back is pressed against the door, and the doorknob touches his hip. He's hungry. His tongue hurts, because Miranda's remark made him tense, and he gulped hot coffee too fast. Give us Brendan's experience in its full complexity.

Becoming someone else can begin with an act as simple—and liberating—as choosing to write from the viewpoint of someone with narrow feet if you yourself have wide feet. You look at the shoes in the window of a store as your character rather than as yourself, and suddenly half a dozen other things become different as well. If you habitually write fiction about someone who is almost you—but who is not alive on the page, because you don't really want to put your own life and personality into stories (or you do but it's too hard), it will be liberating to give your experiences to someone who is less like you. This person who had your experience in the subway will have worse teeth or different taste in clothes, or a body that gains or loses weight differently from yours. I don't mean you should write about a character whose life is dominated by narrow feet. The minor traits will help you sneak up on the important ones. The character may be somewhat like you, but you if you were getting married tomorrow, or about to lose a job, or in some other life-changing situation you're not in. "To whom should this have happened?" is a promising question for turning life into fiction.

I've always had trouble understanding what is sometimes called "characterization." A character isn't someone you construct but someone you feel your way into, gradually sensing what's unique about this person as you might if you found yourself picking up clues as you walked through the house of a stranger. For me, trying to enter a new character—or see someone the character I'm inhabiting sees—seems easier if I make some arbitrary decisions about what's true of this person: in other words, decisions that have nothing to do with the subject matter of the story. Knowing Brendan is religious, please let's not make him calm, philosophical, and meek. Write against type. Make him a brutal Scrabble player who regularly destroys his eight- and ten-year-old daughters' potential triple-word scores.

Looking for characters, think about what they will do in or with the real world. Where is Brendan from? What did he grow up knowing how to do that Miranda can't do? It's often helpful, when looking for a new character, to start by deciding on a minor trait and working outward to the important ones. Trust your intuition. You're picturing someone who's always slapping moisturizer on her forearms? Good, go there. What kind of moisturizer does she like? What about those forearms—does she always wear short sleeves, even in winter? Is she possibly a nurse, who is made to wear short sleeves even though the hospital is cold? If you're writing memoir, start by recalling a real trait this person has that's not relevant to whatever made you decide to write about this person.

Take your imaginative freedom to become someone else a step further. Consider, in your work, becoming someone from a racial or ethnic group you don't belong to, or with a sexual orientation you don't have, and, generally examining parts of life that haven't always received the scrutiny they deserve. Writers of color sometimes feel that they shouldn't write about anything except their own ethnic community. Many white writers don't dare write from the viewpoint of a black person. Writing about people from any marginalized group—whether from their viewpoint or not—can be scary. I've heard white writers say they don't put people of color into their fiction because they're so afraid of being offensive—which results in offensive fiction, depicting a society in which everyone is white. It's also bad for your imagination to put limits on it. You ought to be free to become anyone when you make up a story, and it's terribly sad for you—forgetting the morality of the issue for the moment—if you picture, say, a black man, but revise him—making him white—only because *you're* white, before you begin to type.

Of course, some people think we shouldn't write from the viewpoint of people we're not, especially when it comes to race, sexual orientation, or disability. I disagree. Imaginative freedom, surely, comes first. For a reading in the MFA program in which I teach, I read a story I'd written about a workplace staffed by black people, white people, and Latinos. My protagonist—a foolish though good-hearted young woman—was white, and as the narrator she noted everyone's race, body type—fat or thin—and sexual orientation. I was certain she would be extremely aware of these distinctions, and part of my intention was for the reader of the story to enjoy the distance between the thinking of the character and the stance of the story itself, which (I hope) presented her somewhat ironically. After I read, a black student told me that some people might think my story was racist because I mentioned the race of the characters. He didn't say *he* thought it was racist. Maybe he did. Somehow I suspect he didn't, that he may have enjoyed it but was not sure he should have. I don't know if he specifies the race of people he mentions in his work.

Two of my students of color, over the years, have resisted saying that their characters were, in one case, black and, in the other, Latino. They pointed out that stories about white people don't have to specify—so why should they? I agree, but, as they acknowledged, that meant readers would picture white people—or at least many white readers would. The black student solved the problem by jumping past the word "black," introducing her characters with more detail, maybe about skin tone, body type, hair, country or region of origin: details that made it clear that of course they were black—but made a point about what else they were (as countless stories in which, say, one woman is blond and the other is a green-eyed redhead make you assume they are white). As in life, their being black was only a part of their humanity, but it was a part. The Latino student, last time I saw his work, was still resisting doing more than using Latino last names, but that was interesting too: his stories made the understated point that people who lived lives that weren't culturally distinctive—they didn't speak Spanish, have an *abuelo* in the islands, or eat certain foods—might still be Latino. I've also worked with black students who needed encouragement to make clear simply that their characters were black: they wanted to, but thought they had to somehow work the information in instead of stating it, so they'd write about people's "brown toes" or something similar, and hope you'd figure it out.

Writers of all races sometimes need to pretend to be of a race they are not if they're to be true to the stories they've come up with—and all of us are often afraid. Such a vast variety of subject matter is available to us: we can write about immigrant families whose daily life is suffused in the culture and language of the old country, or immigrant families who scarcely know that their people were once from elsewhere; we can depict people who rarely have interactions in public without being seen by somebody as "other," or people who need to explain that they are "other" because they want it known and it doesn't show. Shouldn't we allow ourselves, all of us, to write about all of this, especially when it's our own, but sometimes when it isn't our own, when a black writer creates a black woman who then falls in love with a man who is, say, half white and half Chinese, and suddenly the story requires that Chapter 3 be from his viewpoint, or even his Chinese father's viewpoint? I think this writer should write the story and then show it to some friend who's Chinese or part Chinese, to see if there's something she got wrong.

Inevitably, stories about multigenerational Jewish families

will mostly or entirely be written by Jews, and stories of multigenerational Haitian families will be written by Haitians or those of Haitian descent. I'm not suggesting that we should take on subject matter of which we know nothing just to prove we have freedom of speech. But we do have freedom of speech, and when it makes sense, we should use it. Let your imagination go where it will; be as brave as you can be, finding out what you may need to know to make your depictions more accurate. And remember that much of experience is universal. When I was learning to write fiction, one day I found myself looking at a black teenage boy coming in my direction on a bicycle. I despaired that I could ever know him well enough to speak for him. I could never speak *for* him, I realized, but I could speak *as* him, at least in some respects. I knew how his rear end felt on the bicycle seat. If I looked over my shoulder, I'd know what he could see. Remember, when writing from the viewpoint of any character, inhabiting that person is, first, physical. You may not know what it's like to experience discrimination or prejudice, but you know how it feels to open a window or scratch a mosquito bite or get caught in the rain. Start there.

When you write about people who have been marginalized—ethnic and racial minorities, people with disabilities, fat people, gay people, and so on—part of the challenge and the thrill is avoiding familiar fictional stereotypes, both in the way you describe your characters and in what happens to them. Whether or not you're a member of a marginalized group, part of your initial intention is probably to combat critical and demeaning stereotypes; if your story requires avaricious Jews or musical black people, you'll take care to make them individuals with complex personalities, and, above all, not the only examples of their group in your story. There are subtler stereotypes to avoid as well, like the all-too-familiar presentation of people from marginalized groups as if their membership in the group is all they think about. Black people walk their dogs or butter their bread without invariably thinking about the history of race in America; gay men and lesbians catch colds that resemble straight people's colds. You can present a person from a marginalized group without making a thematic point of doing so.

When it comes to the shape of a story, there are stereotypes to avoid as well. Books about people from marginalized groups—because of literary history and the history of society—all too easily turn into books about the validity of the category to which the main character belongs. Many fine novels follow a certain broad pattern: First the main character confronts or discovers his or her membership in a group that is discriminated against. Then society's resistance makes the character unsure whether it's really all right to belong to his or her category. And at the end some crisis gives the character the confidence to go on—or society wins and the character is defeated. This structure can be compelling and effective, and I suspect that many of us who have tried writing about members of a group that suffers discrimination have realized at a certain point that the discrimination plot is drawing us in like a whirlpool. But don't use it unless you want to, and as a reader, don't assume the author is using it. I was in a workshop group not long ago in which we all thought a story was about homophobia, which turned out not to be the author's intention. The character was gay, and the other characters resisted him—but homophobia wasn't the reason.

Perhaps the greatest difficulty faced by someone writing about a character from a marginalized group arises when being true to the story and the character means that there must be an unhappy ending that is at least partly the fault of the protagonist. If a character who is a member of a group that's been discriminated against does wrong or spoils something, superficial readers may think the book itself is antifeminist, antiblack, and so on. Yet without the freedom and courage to write the unhappy ending, we don't have the freedom to think about human beings in their full richness, and we're not writing serious books. To write seriously about a member of such groups, we have to get past the need to defend that person's right to be doing whatever it is the character is doing in the first place. Writing such books is a scary project—but an extremely worthy one.

"Well, What Will She Do?"

Among marginalized characters who have been omitted from much fiction, or who have not had important roles when they appear, are women who work, whose work matters to them and the people around them, whose work is not just background but the source of whatever moves the story. For centuries, stories about fictional women—even women who took a serious interest in the world, like Dorothea Brooke in *Middlemarch*—were almost inevitably stories about their relationships with men. In 1908, when Henry James wrote the preface to his 1881 novel *The Portrait of a Lady*, he said he'd wanted to write about a complicated, intelligent young woman "affronting her destiny," not through men but on her own. He acknowledges in the preface that others—Shakespeare and George Eliot, for example—wrote about women who "matter," but what their female characters do centers on action performed by men who matter to the women. But then, James says, having made this plan, he had to answer the question, "Well, what will she *do*?"

We can forgive Henry James, mostly, for assuming that the

woman in his novel, Isabel Archer, would not be a soldier, a lawyer, or a politician. One woman in *The Portrait of a Lady* is a journalist, but James keeps her minor and often makes fun of her. After Isabel rejects a suitor, she imagines that he's gotten over her by busying himself with reform politics, and, says James, "she gave an envious thought to the happier lot of men, who are always free to plunge into the healing waters of action." Isabel yearns to do something that matters, but at the end of the book, she affronts her destiny through choice in her personal life: after traveling away from the evil man she has married, she returns, in solidarity with his power-less daughter. People are still arguing about whether her act is a heroic affront to trouble, or a defeat. A painfully acquired capacity to judge and yet live with evil constitutes her life.

Virginia Woolf, in *A Room of One's Own*—an indispensable essay, arguing that women will write fiction only when we have money of our own and rooms to write in—finds that women's books, over the years, have been limited by discrimination and poverty, as well as by the lack of a tradition, "for we think back through our moth-ers if we are women." After discussing books of the past, she claims to have taken a recent (imaginary) book, *Life's Adventure*, from a shelf and to have found something surprising in it: the sentence "Chloe liked Olivia." She writes, "And I tried to remember any case in the course of my reading where two women are represented as friends." In the imaginary book, women are seen in relation not to men but to one another. Moreover, Chloe and Olivia "shared a lab-oratory together." They are scientists. The book, Woolf says, has flaws and virtues, but as she finishes discussing it, she asserts, "Give her another hundred years."

I think Woolf is asking for, first, books by women that are about women having to do with women. She doesn't speak of lesbian relationships, but surely that's part of it, and these days we do have novels about women's friendships and love (though we need more, and we need them to be marketed to mainstream audiences of men and women alike). Yet it's still hard not to make a book about a woman turn on a relationship with a man. We're all so used to the marriage plot that it sneaks in and takes over, like the discrimination plot in stories about people from marginalized groups.

Woolf is also asking for books about women at work, and it's about time both women and men wrote them, but the same thing happens in many books that mention women's work: work becomes a background to personal life. I want novels and memoirs about women who have a passion for work. (There are short stories about women working, but mostly they're about menial work.) I want these women to be morally complex and interesting, and I want them to do good and harm, to improve or wreck their lives and other people's. Now that women are politicians, doctors, military officers, judges, journalists, and cops, in life we have far more opportunity than Isabel Archer to do harm and good. Yet I find it surprisingly difficult to find and write and advise others in the writing of serious books that show women leading full, demanding lives that affect others, and not just their lovers and families.

Of course, depicting people making a personal connection, or failing to, may be what literature does best. But literature is also good at showing people living through big events, at making public life or history personal. And in many books love and hate take their shape in a mold formed by active life and its results: war separates lovers and families, poverty or wealth makes faithfulness harder, a job presents sexual opportunities, engrossing work wrecks marriages. Or characters must choose between work and love.

Books in which men's work—or men's lust for power, money, and influence—shapes story are much of what we read: all of Shakespeare's tragedies and histories and most of his comedies; books about men traveling in search of adventure, from *Don Quixote* to *Moby-Dick*; and much writing of more recent times. Think of Frank Wheeler in *Revolutionary Road*, trying to be married while struggling ambivalently with his mindless office job; Thomas Sutpen in *Absalom, Absalom!*, mistreating women and doing evil because of his obsession with acquiring the trappings of success in nineteenth-century Mississippi; the characters in *The Great Gatsby*, expressing themselves by acquiring and spending money.

When a novel or memoir focuses on a young person growing into his or her truest self, it can be called a coming-of-age book. It's about work and action as well as sex and love—or, it seems to me, it damn well ought to be. Yet the coming-of-age books about women that fall most readily into one's lap recount the life of a child up to the moment when the girl breaks away from whatever is threatening to squelch her life in advance, when she takes some independent action that points toward a real, complex, adult life in the future—but not in the book. There are dozens. One of my favorites is Dawn Powell's *My Home Is Far Away*, published in 1944 as an "autobiographical novel," about a young girl and her sisters in Ohio, neglected by their lovable father after their mother's death, and treated cruelly by a stepmother, who finally locks the fourteen-year-old heroine—the creative one, the future writer—out of the house. The book ends as the girl gets on a train to go and live her life. Dawn Powell moved to New York and wrote delectably satirical books about cynical people—but this book doesn't follow her there.

In familiar coming-of-age novels about men—*A Portrait of the Artist as a Young Man*, *David Copperfield*, *Great Expectations*—men who often will grow into artists start their adult lives, make mistakes, figure things out, and do harm or good. Howard Sturgis's *Belchamber*, published in 1904, is a coming-of-age novel that actually includes a coming-of-age celebration. It's about a young Englishman, a reluctant peer who abhors the manly activities he's supposed to like, and who is all but explicitly identified as gay. He becomes an unsuccessful grown-up, but he's a grown-up. He makes bad decisions and spoils his life, but that is the right of any fictional character: to be written with sufficient complexity that he or she can fail, if society is as unwelcoming as it would have been in nineteenth-century England to a homosexual lord, and if the character's nature and bad luck wreck what society hasn't already spoiled. This is one book in which the victim of discrimination is allowed to make mistakes.

Literary novels in which young girls grow up to be women and take action that affects others are harder to find. There are fantasy novels about powerful young women, detective stories with female detectives. There's nothing wrong with genre fiction, if that's what you're in the mood for, but its very nature—its delight in adventure, intricate plot, or thrilling departures from reality—keeps it from being a study of character, with the potential for tragedy. For example, P. D. James's novel *An Unsuitable Job for a Woman* is about a young woman who abruptly becomes the head of a detective agency. She works, and her work has good results and bad, but she's not emotionally complex. She doesn't learn or grow.

Women in novels who work are often teachers or governesses, for obvious reasons: Charlotte Brontë's Lucy Snowe, in *Villette*, and Jane Eyre; Jane Austen's Jane Fairfax, in *Emma*. We don't see much of these women's teaching, and they are usually not passionate about their work. More recent novels are likelier to depict women teachers whose work leads to the story. Muriel Spark's *The Prime of Miss Jean Brodie* (1961) is about a complex woman who does both good and harm to her pupils. Another example is Zoë Heller's *What Was She Thinking?*, published in the United Kingdom in 2003 as *Notes on a Scandal*. In the novel an older teacher—a morally complicated woman who gradually reveals her hidden side—tells the story of a young teacher who has an affair with a student. The setting is respected—the staff, procedures, and physical setup of the school are detailed and engrossing—and that makes us far more willing to believe that the sensational plot is real.

There have also been some great novels about women artists. Willa Cather's *The Song of the Lark*, published in 1915, is about an American girl who grows up to be an internationally renowned opera singer. In the later chapters she is a famous soprano singing at the Met in New York, and her art affects her daily life, with difficult rehearsal schedules and late nights. We learn that when she was a young singer abroad, she did not travel home to see her dying mother, because the trip would have prevented her from taking the role that made her career possible. She feels guilty; her friends blame her. Cather doesn't say who is right. This character, like Macbeth or Othello, has the freedom to do what may be wrong.

Now that just about every woman works and some have significant influence, we might expect that a typical contemporary literary novel would show us a woman firing the wrong subordinate and regretting it, or running for Congress and feeling tempted to use negative ads. But though there are plenty of films, TV shows, and genre novels about women with power, it's still not easy to find literary novels in which female characters have ambitions that affect others and are difficult to achieve, lives that are changed by trouble in the world and on the job as well as among the people they know. Often the books I see by student writers are richer and fuller about a woman's girlhood than about her adulthood, or, when concentrating on the life of a young adult woman, are more sure-footed about her love life than about her life at work. In my own writing, I too have found it oddly difficult to center plot on women's work, and easier—to my embarrassment—to write about the professional life of men.

One exception—sort of—is Paule Marshall's 1991 novel, *Daughters*, about Ursa Mackenzie, who grew up in a fictional Caribbean country called Triunion, and now lives in Manhattan. The novel recounts a couple of months in which Ursa breaks up with a boyfriend, gets a job, may or may not be pregnant despite an abortion, and travels to the island where she grew up and where her father is an important political figure. There are not many pages in which Ursa is at her job—one wonderful chapter—but work and the personal qualities that lead to good work shape the book, and the work life of every female character matters: Ursa's best friend is a vice president at Metropolitan Life, her mother is a former schoolteacher, her father's mistress manages a hotel. Ursa is hired to work on a big study that will benefit poor people in a mostly black town in New Jersey. I see why the job gets only one chapter (though I want more): Marshall is writing primarily about the similarities—especially powerlessness—in the political life of black people in the United States and in the Caribbean, so Ursa's job is in the book partly to be compared to the situation she finds at home. The book's climax comes about when Ursa performs an action in Triunion that is unrelated to her job, yet it draws on the ideals and confidence that work has given her. Even though what she does will hurt her loved father's career, she takes action that will spoil a secret government plan to destroy a tract of loved and economically essential rural land. Ursa affronts her destiny.

It's not hard to guess the reasons that writing such books may be difficult. For many centuries a novel about a woman doctor (for example) was so unlikely that when it became possible to write one, it still seemed unlikely. When we have written such books, because the carrying-out of work by women is still a recent phenomenon, often they are books arguing that it's right for women to work, instead of assuming it and moving on from there. In George Gissing's 1893 novel *The Odd Women*, Rhoda Nunn teaches young women secretarial skills so they can break into a profession that was at that time all male. It's a book in which women most certainly work, and in which their work generates at least part of the story, but it exists to make the point—it's an argument more than an exploration of character.

There's nothing wrong with such books—they are essential—but habit comes into play: once we expect that a book about a woman who works will not be about what she does but whether she should do it, it's hard to think up a story that doesn't take us in that direction. It can be tempting to make the woman emotionally disabled: can she deal with her problems and do the job? The result, again, is a book not about working but about whether work will be done. Writing any novel is hard, but it may be easier to write a book in which, at the end, someone overcomes her difficulties and makes a single brave gesture in the direction of a meaningful future, than one in which someone takes action all along.

I suspect that working women and any characters who belong to marginalized groups, when they're in genre fiction, films, TV shows, or comic strips, are likelier than similar characters in literary fiction to have the power to make mistakes, because those forms usually have happy endings. When we dare to give characters who in past times weren't allowed to act the freedom to come to bad ends and make tragic mistakes, we'll be past the barrier I sense in serious literature.

As in so much of this business, we must all be braver. What's the worst that can happen?

PART III

Stories and Books:
Start to Finish

CHAPTER 6

Recognize Stories, Envision Books

What's a Story? Grace Paley's "A Conversation with My Father"

How do pieces of writing, assuming they're good—the characters feel alive, the events seem significant, the language is sharp and original—convince us that they are *whole*, so that we start reading, continue, then come to the last words, stop, let out a held breath, and agree that, yes, what had begun is now finished?

It's hard to write something that will call forth that satisfied sigh, hard to turn a pile of pages into a work of art. How do we know when to stop? What is *enough* for a story? When writing an entire book, how can we keep our heads clear while making choices and decisions about a book's worth of characters and story?

Taste varies, and some "short short" stories may seem complete to one reader but incomplete to the next. Still, the popularity of "sudden fiction" or "flash fiction"—a story that is sometimes just a few words long—suggests that there is an entity most of us recognize as "a story," and that what makes it a story has nothing to do with length. We may argue about particular examples, but even people who prefer to get lost in a story, emerging an hour or more later, may agree that, yes, that fifty-two-word thing that just ran by was indeed a *story*; and, on the other hand, even the laconic authors of short short stories may look at their fifty-word creations and think, "Nope, not done yet," then add a few words and it's finished.

We all seem to recognize that a story implies, if it doesn't include, two or three events. Whatever is going on at the start of a story, the narrative generally takes at least two steps away from it: a situation changes and then changes back, or changes further; a person conceives a desire or fear and then confronts its embodiment—and then what's feared or desired does or doesn't appear, or appears in an unexpected way, or something else entirely happens. In a story, that is, a few events happen—and the last one is sufficiently decisive that it feels, well, like an end.

To understand what we're talking about in the simplest terms, we may find it helpful to look at an atypical story: "A Conversation with My Father," by Grace Paley, from her second collection, *Enormous Changes at the Last Minute*, which came out in 1974. A father (Paley says in a note that her other characters are fictional but the father is her father) demands to know why his daughter no longer writes what he calls "a simple story": "Just recognizable people and then write down what happened to them next." The narrator doesn't want to do that, never has wanted to, because plot "takes all hope away." She tells the reader, "Everyone, real or invented, deserves the open destiny of life."

Then, to satisfy him or defy him, she makes up a story: A woman takes drugs in solidarity with her addicted son, who then gets clean and has nothing more to do with her. The father objects. She has left out detail—the woman's appearance and background. For him, the nature of the person is all—he wants to know how such choices could come about, what led to them? The daughter expands the story, and in the second version, though she doesn't seem to care much about finding a background that would explain the woman's life, there's more feeling, more detail. The father is unconvinced. He talks about what a tragedy this story is, and the daughter counters that, no, there's always hope; the woman doesn't get her son back, but she ends up working in a drug clinic, where her experience is valued. The father insists that the daughter is denying the tragedy: this woman could not change. "When will you look it in the face?" he asks as the story ends.

Father and daughter argue about both the structure and the content of the story she makes up. About structure the father is right. The first version of the story doesn't really tell "what happened next," though it moves along in time; the son is an addict, and then he is no longer an addict: "After a while, for a number of reasons, the boy gave it all up and left the city and his mother in disgust." Stories tell what happened next in some way that suggests that there's a connection between the two events. If a child builds a sand castle and rain washes it away, that's not enough. But if the parent, initially, warns that it's likely to rain, the whole thing comes to life: now building the sand castle is an act of defiance; the rain is a cruel confirmation of the child's helplessness.

The daughter's second version of the story about the mother and son makes more of his change (he meets a girl who is into health food, and is converted), but, putting aside the comedy in both versions—Paley is teasing not just her father but the reader—there is admittedly something structurally incomplete about the story—a problem that does not, in fact, occur in Grace Paley's actual stories, whatever her father thinks. In the bits of fiction the daughter offers the father, Grace Paley is writing parodies of her own stories, not examples.

The father fails to see what she's up to. Grace Paley's stories don't trivialize life, though everything is at least a little funny and her characters find surprising ways out of bad situations. There is plenty of heartbreak, plenty of intensity—but, indeed, always "the open destiny of life."

The story itself, however—"A Conversation with My Father"—is complete, and what completes it is that this argument about literature takes place as the father is dying. The very first sentence is "My father is eighty-six years old and in bed." The daughter, she tells us, has "promised the family to always let him have the last word when arguing." At the end the father takes "oxygen tubes out of his nostrils" to accuse his daughter: "Jokes, jokes again," he says. The story takes place in a short period of time—or possibly on several occasions, each just a conversation—but in it something shifts, maybe in the daughter, maybe only in the reader. The story is about love, about arguing as a way of loving, and about death: whatever story the daughter writes can't keep her father alive or make him well again; they both know that, and by the end the reader knows it too. He wants her to imitate Chekhov and Turgenev—take on, I guess, the great tragic themes, give them their dignified due. But all the while, as he takes oxygen tubes out of his nostrils to speak, she is giving a tragic theme its due: this is a story of love and separation between parent and child, more fully realized—because more happens and because we know the people better—than the story-within-the-story of the mother and son, who never come to life. In *this* story many things happen: the father's initial request, the invention of the story, the critique, the second version, the new critique—all as he lies on his deathbed. Father and daughter are using their last moments together to argue about literature, about tragedy.

In a story that's complete, enough happens—however slight the incidents may be—that we don't know the end and want to know the end. There is enough new incident not necessarily to change a character (some people never change) but to change the reader: we start someplace, go a distance, and return, or go a distance and arrive. Sometimes the character changes, but in a complete story the reader always changes—if only changing position: we lean back, saying, "Ahhh." Or we sit up straight near the end, realize we were wrong, and relax again. Or we sag in our chairs, a little bored, thinking we see what the author is up to—and then sit up with a jerk. We go through something.

Tillie Olsen's "I Stand Here Ironing"

Tillie Olsen's only complete book of fiction was a collection of four short stories, *Tell Me a Riddle*. It was published in 1961, but I didn't find it until the mid-seventies—around the time I found Grace Paley—when I picked up a dilapidated copy in a New Haven bookstore. It was the period in my life when I was looking after three young children and writing poetry, wishing I could also write fiction.

Olsen's stories are about ordinary life—children, parents, old people, and the struggle to put up with one another and try to live decently. They don't have surprising endings, only endings that show how the difficult truths that the author has laid out are even more true than you might have expected, but that love is also more possible than you thought. Her characters are likelier to say the wrong thing than the right. They hurt one another, but only death makes anyone disappear from anyone else's life. Her stories are political without being preachy, without sacrificing the particular person to the general truth. This all suited me, and before long I began writing my own stories, though it took me years to write a story anyone could publish. In some ways Olsen wasn't the best model. Not much happens in her stories; imitating them, I wrote stories in which *nothing* happened, which is very different.

"I Stand Here Ironing," the first story, consists of an internal monologue: a mother, ironing, imagines talking to a guidance counselor or social worker who has asked her to come in and discuss her oldest daughter. It begins, "I stand here ironing, and what you asked me moves tormented back and forth with the iron." The story consists of what she imagines saying. As she describes her daughter she uses sharply observed detail, often emotional and impressionistic, not just descriptive ("She blew shining bubbles of sound" or "a clogged weeping that could not be comforted"), but I think much of the appeal of the story, Olsen's most famous, is that the mother is defensive, angry, and regretful all at once; she blames herself and the society in which she raised her daughter equally. The girl, Emily, has had a hard time, and the mother is unsentimental, even grim. We learn about Emily's troubles, but we also learn that she's lively and funny. She's a comedian who performs successfully at school events.

Then, as her mother continues ironing and imagining a conversation, Emily herself "runs up the stairs two at a time with her light graceful step, and I know she is happy tonight. Whatever it was that occasioned your call did not happen today." Emily's vitality breaks into her mother's interior monologue: the daughter's entrance is the only actual occurrence besides ironing. Emily teases her mother, puts together a meal for herself, and then jokingly says something despairing as she goes to bed, and the mother tells the reader (or the social worker she is imagining), "I cannot endure it tonight." She will not go in to discuss her daughter, she says. The story ends,

Let her be. So all that is in her will not bloom—but in how many does it? There is still enough left to live

by. Only help her to know—help make it so there is
cause for her to know—that she is more than this dress
on the ironing board, helpless before the iron.

This story is visually complex. In our minds as we read we see
the mother in her kitchen with her iron and ironing board—and
Emily coming in—and, as if through the mother, we also picture
the listening social worker (who will never hear all this), and
beyond them we see what the mother is describing: Emily as a
baby, a child, a teenager. You could call it a static story in which the
ending is simply an image—and ending a story with an image is
usually not as powerful as ending it with an event—but we've been
seeing that iron go back and forth all along, as the mother talks, so
it's more than an inert comparison: we have the horrifying brief
image of a girl being ironed flat. Moreover, the story is suspenseful:
we wait to find out whether the mother will tell all this to the professional person, who may (or may not) help. In one sense nothing
happens in this story, but there is plenty of uncertainty as we read
on to find out what happened to Emily in the past, and what the
mother may do about it. Her decision to do nothing, along with
what she says, constitutes an event that matters. I think at the end
of this story we sorrowfully nod our heads. This mother is probably right.

Most new writers I meet say they have trouble with plot. They
seem to mean that they can come up with characters and situations—
two unhappy sisters with a sick mother; an office in which the boss
is unfair—but not the kind of event that unsettles the situation and
sets a story in motion, the moment in time that can be seen as the
beginning of some kind of shift. They have the habit of thinking in
terms of "plot" on the one hand and "characters" on the other. "I
can't do plot," people wail at me, as if their people existed apart from

it, as if plot were something to add. But plot is often almost nothing. It's whatever keeps the reader moving forward, whatever keeps the reader from thinking the publisher omitted some pages. The pre-cipitating event in "I Stand Here Ironing" is only remembered: it's the invitation from the social worker to come and talk, which becomes more noteworthy to the reader when we see Emily's vital-ity and charm. A possible opening occurs—and the mother rejects it. Most stories have more eventful events than that—I don't think you should *aim* for subtle events—but what I failed to see, for years, was that the subtle events in stories like Olsen's and Paley's are still events, and are essential.

In a recent workshop I taught, one student's story was about a man in his seventies who owns a restaurant in which one thing after another goes wrong. The man is afraid of sabotage, and the reader too thinks someone may be making trouble on purpose. Then health department inspectors show up, and there are so many violations that the man's son gets involved, and then learns from the staff that his father's memory is failing; that's the reason for the trouble. The son must take control of his formerly indepen-dent, competent dad: the story comes to a moving conclusion. In discussions of a story in workshop, I usually begin by asking the students to name its strengths. I knew that they would speak of the qualities that made this story *good*—psychological verisimili-tude, characters we cared about, telling language. So this time I spoke first: I praised the arrival of the health department inspec-tors. I suspected that otherwise the incident wouldn't be men-tioned. It was just a few unadorned sentences—but they made the story work. This is what I meant by saying, at the start of this book, that I'm writing not about what makes fiction good but about what makes it possible.

Later in her life Tillie Olsen published, as a short story, "Requa I," the first part of a novella that was never completed. The story was printed in a journal in 1970 and then in *Best American Short Stories*, and it's included in a collection of Olsen's work published in 2013, *Tell Me a Riddle, Requa I, and Other Works*. With almost no explanatory narrative, it recounts, through dialogue and the characters' thoughts, the relationship between a man and his thirteen-year-old nephew in 1932. The uncle has taken the orphaned boy to live with him in a boardinghouse. The boy is inert with grief; the well-meaning uncle is baffled and increasingly impatient. Then, slowly, there are tiny changes in what the boy does. He is healing. Story is a relative matter. In an adventure story the slight changes in the way this boy and his uncle live would count as stasis. In this story slight changes are as striking as dramatic plot events elsewhere.

Edward P. Jones's "The Sunday Following Mother's Day"

We all know why suspenseful stories with dramatic conclusions are stories. But stories like those we've just considered, which really work the same way—life becomes unsettled and eventually is resolved—are harder to describe as a series of events leading to other events, though they are. So are long, apparently inconclusive stories like "The Sunday Following Mother's Day," from Edward P. Jones's first book, *Lost in the City*. One minor reason I love this story is that the author gets away with including two characters named Maddie and Madeleine, and *three* named Sam. The story begins with a plain statement of fact: "When Madeleine Williams was four years old and her brother Sam was ten, their father killed their mother one night in early April." Jones tells us immediately that no one would ever find out why this murder occurred, so we know not to expect that the story is going in *that* direction. From the second paragraph we occasionally look back at events from the vantage point of Madeleine after she has grown up and gone to Columbia University. As an adult she reads all she can about the murder. The story describes in detail the events just after the murder, summarizes most of the next twenty years, and finally slows way down: the last five pages are about one day—a day that turns out to have more to do with race, class, forgiveness, and friendship than murder. By this time Madeleine is married and has a son, also named Sam, who is mentally disabled and in an institution.

Samuel, the murderer, has now been released from prison and has been writing his daughter loving letters. On the Sunday following Mother's Day, when her husband happens to be away, Madeleine is about to go visit her son in the institution when her father comes to her house, appearing for the first time since he murdered her mother all those years ago, and persuades her to let him drive her. They arrive, another family befriends them, and then a series of hapless accidents puts Madeleine in that family's company for hours. They idealize the disabled children and cloyingly pretend to impossible friendship. It's unspoken but obvious that the institution takes inadequate care of its poor, black residents, which makes the family Madeleine meets even more disturbing. She realizes that these people are like her father: countrified, simple black people—people decidedly unlike her. A less complex author would make the reader reject Madeleine's snobbish loathing for these people and her father, but here everyone is culpable and everyone is right.

A long-ago murder has nothing to do with what's important at the end of the story: what seems to make a difference then are dilapidated cars, clumsy social life, and embarrassing, foolish civilities. The story carries the reader away from the murder, resisting a simple view of tragedy and leaving that situation unresolved. A tragic ending would require one of the children to kill the father, or the father to murder again. This story becomes comedy. It moves from its opening and then returns to it, resolves it somehow—but resolves it by rejecting it. The stark question that has seemed to motivate the children's lives—can we forgive the murderer of our mother if he's our father?—vanishes in the inconvenient detail of the day-to-day. The story slows down, and looking at anything slowly makes it complicated.

So there are many ways to write a story in which something happens and something else happens, and it's the "something else"—a new thing that breaks into the story, often on page 3 or 4—that frequently distinguishes professional writers' stories from the work of beginners: there's an initial problem, and then there's a new, unexpected person or problem or complexity, as if the author has looked around and thought, "What else is going on here? What else might happen here?" Once there has been an event or several events, then something happens, finally, that is of enough magnitude that we feel that a *story* has occurred. It sounds obvious, but if you think of it that way—a story feels like a story—then you'll be able to judge whether the resolutions and solutions and tragedies and uncertainties that you come up with have both psychological rightness—fictional truth—and the requisite force.

A Novel That Never Was Written

When I began writing my first novel, the task seemed so intimidating that I didn't tell anyone what I was doing for months, and spoke of it as "the thing." During those years I helped serve lunch in a soup kitchen every Monday, and a distinguished psychoanalyst also volunteered. One Monday, as we passed trays down the line of volunteers and staff members, each adding a scoop of meat, potatoes, or vegetables, someone called to me, "Aren't you a writer? What are you writing?"

"Well," I said, stopping to concentrate on a scoop of mashed potatoes. "Well." I had actually never said it before. Another scoop. "I'm writing . . . well, I'm writing . . . um, I'm writing . . . a novel."

The psychoanalyst murmured sympathetically, "So it's come to that."

In subsequent years I've learned that anxiety about writing a first novel or a book-length memoir is common. How the hell do you write something *that* long? If a story is a couple of incidents, one final and decisive, what's a book? Two hundred incidents, one final and decisive? How do you even keep track of the damn thing? My first novel eventually did get written, somehow, but many others are never finished.

Tillie Olsen, the author of "I Stand Here Ironing," was born Tillie Lerner in 1912 to secular Jewish immigrants from Russia in Omaha, Nebraska. Her parents were leftist activists. Tillie Lerner never finished high school or went to college, but she was a serious reader, and in her twenties, during the Great Depression, she began writing poems and a novel. She married young, became a Communist, had a daughter, moved to California. In 1934, part of her unfinished novel was published in the *Partisan Review*, and at the very time that Lerner was jailed for support of a longshoremen's strike, the *New Republic*—in a story about proletarian literature—called her novel excerpt "a work of early genius." Publishers went searching for this Tillie Lerner and found her in jail. She was offered money, asked to write about her political life, offered a contract for a novel. Every writer's fantasy. But she doesn't seem to have taken the distant world of publishing very seriously, though she was glad to get money. She wrote an article about the strike and implied in a letter to Bennett Cerf, founder of Random House, that her novel was almost finished. Her biographer, Panthea Reid, in *Tillie Olsen: One Woman, Many Riddles* records that she signed a contract with Macmillan, then agreed to sign with Random House. Macmillan eventually released her, and she signed with Random House for a $500 advance and 15 percent of royalties, very high for the time. She promised to send eight chapters, and in the months that followed, she sent two, admitting that she hadn't actually worked on the novel for two years. Her old notes were chaotic. She was sick several times, her marriage ended, and her life, working with other activists, was full of turmoil.

Though her biographer doesn't say this, it seems clear that there was never any reason to think Tillie Lerner was writing a novel or would finish one—but the publishers wanted a novel from her, and she and they tacitly agreed to pretend that one would appear. In 1935 and 1936 she planned chapters and periodically asked for more money and received it, for a total of $1,200. She sent in no more writing. She was working full time for the Communist Party, and it must have been hard to believe that she could do more for the world by sitting alone writing and rewriting fiction than by going out and fighting for social change. In her article about the longshoremen's strike, which is included in the 2013 collection of her work, she describes a day when the police violently attacked the strikers. She was not on the picket line: she was in Communist Party headquarters, typing, she says, while horrors took place outside and ambulances rushed by: "And I sit there, making a metallic little pattern of sound in the air, because that is all I can do, because that is what I am supposed to do." This doesn't sound like someone who was likely to give up working for the party—even if all she did for it was type—and sit at home for months writing a novel.

Also, my guess is that Tillie Lerner didn't know *how* to write a novel—as we've noted, it's not obvious—and resisted the combination of imaginative freedom and consecutive thinking it would require. She had written articles for a party newsletter and several pieces of journalism but, not having been to college, would have had little experience planning and completing other pieces of writing, and she was a perfectionist.

She began living with Jack Olsen, another Communist. They had three more daughters, and married during the forties, when he was in the army, so she'd receive the benefits military wives were entitled to. She then became Tillie Olsen.

In 1954, when Tillie Olsen was forty-two, she got in touch with a writer named Arthur Foff, with whom one of her daughters was studying at San Francisco State College. She showed him a draft of the story that eventually became "I Stand Here Ironing," and he let her into his class. As his student, she finished that story and made notes for the others that would later be published in *Tell Me a Riddle*. Foff encouraged her to apply for a fellowship at Stanford, and Wallace Stegner phoned to offer her a fellowship that included attending classes. There she studied with the novelist Richard Scowcroft, and over the next three years, she completed the other stories in *Tell Me a Riddle*. Mostly she still couldn't write, and Scowcroft recorded that she cried during their conferences. But she published the four stories in magazines and got a contract for the collection. Publishers fought over her again, and now Viking offered her a contract for a novel. She promised various novels to more than one publisher, but never completed any.

Finally, her husband found two envelopes containing the incomplete novel from the thirties, which had been lost. Tillie Olsen couldn't finish it, but she was able to make sense of the fragments of the early chapters, and they were published as *Yonnondio: From the*

Thirties in 1974. Its harrowing, gorgeous, sensitively written chapters recount the childhood of Mazie Holbrook. Her father works in the Wyoming mines, then becomes an unsuccessful tenant farmer. He finds unsafe work in the Omaha sewers, then gets a job in a slaughterhouse, where he is in danger from scalding water. The story is an indictment of injustice, callousness, and lack of opportunity, a chronicle of the Great Depression—and also a sharply observed account of children growing up. It is even more fervent in its outrage than *Tell Me a Riddle* but no less exact and irresistible in depicting life moment by moment. It breaks off with a note that begins, "Reader, it was not to have ended here."

Back in the thirties, Tillie Lerner had sent a plan to Random House outlining the novel she intended to write. Editors there pointed out to one another that she had done nothing more than enumerate one disaster after another. They tried to keep from criticizing her so as not to discourage her, but Cerf wrote her that she might consider giving her main character "a few good breaks here and there." The plan stayed at Random House, and when she was working on *Yonnondio* in the seventies, Olsen didn't have it. Panthea Reid includes it in an appendix.

Yonnondio, insofar as it exists, *isn't* just a recitation of disasters, though there are plenty of those. The author is seduced by the look, sound, and smell of things, the psychological feel of whatever is going on, and we have the thrill of reading something true about life—which is a happy experience, even when we are reading about suffering. In *Yonnondio* there is a *little* too much insistence on how bad everything is, but I imagine that Tillie Olsen would have written the rest with her usual clear eye and sense of language, her usual insight into human psychology. As a series of pages and paragraphs, the book would have worked, as the early chapters do.

Still, the plan suggests that it might not have worked as a whole book, a novel. I'm doubtful not because of the many disasters, but because Olsen is thinking not about what her characters will *do*, only about what they will experience—what will happen to them— and what these happenings will feel like. She projects a series of descriptions, almost tableaus, without actions resulting at least in part from earlier actions. The book would have lacked the events that keep a novel from becoming a series of static portraits. It seems that her intention, in each chapter, is to demonstrate to readers what situations mean emotionally, not to start up uncertainties in the reader's mind. Here's a piece of the plan that outlines a chapter she never wrote:

> The City: With Will in the reformatory for running away. School and how alien it and the kids are. Mazie friendship for Ellen her cousin and their dreams together. The neighborhood, the poverty, the sense of being a burden and Jerry bitter tongue, the men around. The work for room and board, and falling asleep in school over her lessons, the shame . . .

She would have produced a series of gloriously alive, difficult moments, as she did in her stories, which work because the passage of time, and subtle shifts and arrivals and departures, as well as undramatic but real sources of suspense—like the question of whether Emily's mother will go and talk to the counselor—provide forward motion. But she'd probably have needed more for a book; she'd have needed characters with desires, who try to act.

When she did write parts of the novel, she didn't like them, and she may have been correct that they didn't work. She needed friends and books, help making up if not a plot, at least a series of forward-looking episodes that would carry a reader along. Then—well, maybe nothing would have helped, but *maybe* she'd have liked what she was writing and found the courage to continue.

Olsen did better as a spokesperson for her ideas. She was a political leftie all her life and, apparently, took delight in almost any disruption of established order. In her last decades she was a vocal feminist celebrity who regularly used more than her allotted time as a public speaker and jumped from subject to subject, resisting all demands for coherence and logic. Her passionate talks about feminism and the thirties inspired many. When she was invited to Yale, a mile from my house, I heard her speak. She spontaneously sang "Brother, Can You Spare a Dime?" (maybe she always spontaneously sang it, I don't know), and I was smitten. She died in 2007.

The story of Tillie Olsen is sad, despite the existence of those amazing stories and the fragment *Yonnondio*, as well as a nonfiction book she wrote called *Silences*—which, tellingly, is about how women find it hard to write—and despite her years as a feminist role model. Her youth wasn't wasted: there were good reasons (something her biographer, who is unfortunately highly critical of her subject, doesn't seem to grasp) why an ethical young woman might have devoted her time to the Communist Party in the 1930s. Still, the silence is tragic: there should have been more fiction.

Imagining a Novel

My guess is that novels come about in one of two ways. One is when the original impulse is an idea for an action that will be at the center of the book (a crime, an accident, a misunderstanding), an idea that comes trailing possible subsequent actions—or actions that lead up to it—like strands of mozzarella off a pizza.

Although writing such a novel has its own difficulties, the outline of the story—what draws us in, what makes us keep reading, what complicates matters, what resolves them—will be fairly clear.

But maybe you don't want to or can't write that kind of novel, the kind that turns on a dramatic action that comes to mind first. For me, and maybe for you, a novel doesn't start up in the mind as an action; it starts as a person in a situation. One novel started in my mind as an ending: four women who know one another each go into different stalls of a women's room, to be alone for the first time in hours, after something huge has happened. I needed to write a book that would explain their pleasure in that moment of solitude—how the main character, especially, finally has a chance to think, and what she thinks. Feeling my way backward, I slowly imagined a series of events that would lead to this moment. If you start writing novels this way, your musings have to do with the actions and large questions that might best lead to the feelings and nature of people in the situation you have in mind, and bring them to the place where you want them to end.

Or you may first conceive of a novel by imagining people and how they know one another. You've written a story, and a friend or teacher says, "This could be a novel!" or your story is published and an agent writes to you and says, "Do you have a *novel*? Is this story part of a *novel*?" You think, why not? You could go on forever about these two brothers . . . the time they got lost, the time their sister fell in love. . . .

If you think first of characters and relationships, whether your story is based on real people or not, you may think up incident after incident, but maybe not a central one large enough to carry the book and set it up for a conclusion. You may have to struggle for quite a while to decide what matters most to these brothers, what could take them to the next place in their lives.

In Chapter 7 we'll go into more detail about all this. All we need to agree on right now is that in a novel some large thing needs to happen. Maybe we don't write mysteries about crime—but *all* novels are mysteries about crime in one way or another, though the crime may be kissing the wrong man or spoiling a friendship, and the mystery may be something like "Will this character fix her life?"

You may not know the ending, but you may know what the ending will be about—either a marriage or a breakup, either an accomplishment or a failure, either a moment of new mutual comprehension or renewed hopeless enmity. It may take you many weeks or months to think of events that will take you to the ending   and let you find out what exactly it is—but after a while you'll have a wisp of a novel.

And then what? Novelists are often asked, "Do you use an outline?" Probably not. I suspect that only predictable fiction, with formulas instead of lifelike characters, could be completely planned in advance. People who make up imaginative stories are often uncomfortable with strict logic and rigid planning. What we're good at is using free association and other sloppy techniques that encourage our thoughts to run easily, so, feeling our way, we can sense what small but believable, emotionally true thing will happen next. An outline would be too rational for most of us, and for the way we happen upon story. Is there a way to use intuition and feeling along with reason (a flying kite tugged now and then by a good stout string) to organize the large elements in a book?

The Quarry for Middlemarch

A few years ago, in an exhibit of manuscripts collected by the poet Amy Lowell at Harvard's Houghton Library, I saw a small notebook identified as the "quarry" George Eliot used when she wrote one of my favorite novels, *Middlemarch*—which, as you probably know, is about a fictional Midlands English town and especially two people in it, Dorothea Brooke and Tertius Lydgate. They are ambitious and idealistic, wanting to improve life for others, but they marry the wrong people: they are both powerful and smart, but at times foolish. This novel is a grand statement about how hard it is to become the person you dream of being—someone who does good work—how firmly the world will oppose you, but how love can make a difference, while its absence is hell. Even with someone to love who shares your ideals and understands your thoughts, the narrow prejudices of provincial life may make you fail. *Middlemarch* was published in serial form in 1871 and 1872, and as a book in 1874, but it takes place in 1830 and '31, just before the passage of the Reform Act enlarged the English electorate and made the country more democratic.

The notebook I saw under glass was open to a page on which Eliot had written down a list of the scenes in the fifth section of her novel. It was a stunning moment: I was watching George Eliot figure out her book. I pulled out a notebook of my own and wrote down everything I saw. Some lines were crossed out, and some were hard to read. I copied "Mr. Casaubon dies. Brooke stands and falls. Embarrassment of Lydgate. Raffles comes on the scene. Scandal in Middlemarch"—about twenty such short summaries. I noticed that they all had to do with action, with event, not with feeling—George Eliot knew she didn't have to remind herself what the characters would feel.

The *Oxford English Dictionary* defines "quarry" as "an open-air excavation from which stone for building or other purposes is obtained by cutting, blasting, or the like." In other words, a quarry makes what's shaped and functional out of what's haphazard. And it's where you'd go digging. George Eliot produced a few other "quarries" besides the one for *Middlemarch*—two for her novel *Romola*, one written in Italian, and one for a novel she never wrote— but the one for *Middlemarch* is the most detailed and complicated. In 1950 the University of California Press published it, edited by Anna Theresa Kitchel, and I was able to borrow her edition.

The quarry is in two parts. Eliot wrote from the beginning to the middle of the notebook, then turned it upside down and backward and started again from what had been the back cover. Harvard owns the quarry and will let you see a facsimile on the Web; the second part is upside down. The first part consists of notes Eliot made when she read about medicine as it was practiced in the 1830s, to help her write about Tertius Lydgate, who's a young doctor. The second part is her plan for the book.

Eliot also kept journals, not very detailed. She records trips, visitors, a few words about her writing, and names the books, in several languages, she is reading. She often mentions having a headache or losing a day to illness. She speaks of how happy she is with George Henry Lewes, the man she lived with for many years, mentioning "our growing love."

In November of 1868 Eliot writes in the journal, "The return of this Saint Cecilia's day finds me in better health than has been usual with me in these last six months. But I am not yet engaged in any work that makes a higher life for me—a life that is young and grows, though in my other life I am getting old and decaying. It is a day for resolves, and determination."

A month later, on New Year's Day, 1869, she writes, "I have set myself many tasks for the year—I wonder how many will be accomplished?" Along with some poems, she plans "A Novel called Middlemarch." On January 23: "I have made a little way in constructing my new Tale." Six months later—the next time she refers to it—she is "writing an introduction to Middlemarch." A week after that she "meditated characters for Middlemarch." She records beginning the book on August 2, but she began with a section that comes second in the finished novel. On September 1 she again "meditated characters and conditions for Middlemarch which stands still in the beginning of Chapter III." Then, on September 10: "I have achieved little during the last week except reading on Medical subjects." The next day she writes:

> I do not feel very confident that I can make anything satisfactory of Middlemarch. I have need to remember that other things which have been accomplished by me, were begun under the same cloud. G. has been reading Romola again, and expresses profound admiration. This is encouraging. *At p.50—end of Chapter III.*

A couple of weeks later: "As to my work, *im Stiche gerathen*"— German for "stuck." And three days after that:

> It is worth while to record my great depression of spirits, that I may remember one more resurrection from the pit of melancholy. And yet what love is given to me!—what abundance of good I possess. All my circumstances are blessed; and the defect is only in my own organism. Courage and effort!

During these months, Lewes's son was staying with them. He'd been living in Africa, and arrived sick. Eliot briefly records his ups and downs day by day and then his death, after which she didn't write in her journal for seven months. When she started again, turning the book over and writing toward the beginning, as with the quarry, she speaks of writing poems, traveling, and being ill. *Middlemarch* is still stalled.

George Eliot, a prolific and great novelist, suffered from the troubles that touch every writer's life. She was sick, depressed, unable to figure out what to write next. Though she lived happily with her partner (despite societal disapproval because he was married, though he and his wife had agreed to an open marriage and his wife had children with another man), love couldn't save them from sorrow and loss. Beginning writers sometimes think there is something wrong with them because troubles like these hold them back. Obviously not.

Finally, on December 2, 1870—sixteen months after she began writing *Middlemarch*—Eliot writes in her journal:

> I am experimenting in a story, which I began without any very serious intention of carrying it out lengthily. It is a subject which has been recorded among my possible themes ever since I began to write fiction, but will probably take new shapes in the development. I am today at p.44.

On December 31, she writes:

> I have written only 100 pages—good printed pages—of a story which I began about the opening of November, and at present mean to call 'Miss Brooke.' Poetry halts just now.
>
> In my private lot I am unspeakably happy, loving, and beloved. But I am doing little for others.

At some point the story she refers to became part of the novel—it is the story of Dorothea Brooke, one of the two central characters of the novel. After that, in subsequent entries in 1871 and 1872, she records progress on *Middlemarch*—and then its publication and success.

At the start of the book, Tertius Lydgate has recently moved to Middlemarch to take over another doctor's practice. The chapters she was stuck on, I suppose, are versions of the ones that exist as the second of the novel's eight books, in which Lydgate starts up his practice and tries to make a place for himself in the town, falling in love with a beautiful but difficult woman, Rosamond Vincy. He has to take a stand in a decision made by the board of directors of a new hospital, which he will run, and his decision makes enemies for him. Thus the conflicts in Lydgate's story begin: struggles concerning love, work, and money.

The story "Miss Brooke," which Eliot began so casually after being stuck for months, became not just part of *Middlemarch* but the part that begins it, and which many of us remember most clearly when we think of this book. Eliot wrote poems and a story because she couldn't write her novel—and then the story turned out to be the salvation of the novel. Dorothea Brooke is an idealistic, intense, intellectually curious young woman who marries a cold scholar whose life has been wasted on trivia. She believes he is brilliant and hopes to help him with his work—and then she realizes the truth. Like George Eliot as she began that part of the story, Dorothea is unhappy that she does nothing for others. As her story plays out, she becomes acquainted with her husband's cousin Will Ladislaw—and their story eventually dominates the book. So George Eliot had to wait to write her book until she realized that a story she already had in mind belonged with the one she was writing. When we read *Middlemarch* now, the linking of the two stories seems inevitable.

~

Research and reading may be invaluable in writing a novel, not only because they keep us from making mistakes, but because they may suggest story. An actual quarry has plenty of rock in it that will never be cut up and made into anything, and George Eliot, as she read about medicine—preparing herself to write about a young doctor practicing forty years earlier—read widely and wrote down what interested her, not knowing whether she'd use it or not. Sometimes she didn't. In the quarry she noted controversies about such issues as how much doctors could charge and whether they might dispense drugs. Lydgate, a reformer, advocates new medical practices and refuses to dispense drugs, and the local doctors think he's an incompetent snob.

Eliot also noted the changing understanding of typhus and typhoid fever, which had been considered one disease. Research took place in Paris, and we learn that Lydgate studied there.

Early in the book a young man, Fred Vincy, comes down with typhoid fever. Another Middlemarch doctor sees Fred but doesn't take his illness seriously. Lydgate is called in, realizes what's wrong, and treats it—and in the course of his many visits, he confers with Fred's sister Rosamond, and they fall in love; she is the woman he marries. The facts about typhoid fever that Eliot had written down enable her not just to write accurately about the disease, but also to advance the story. We don't know whether an idea for the plot came first and the information about typhoid second, or whether information she found suggested what might happen. But since she didn't use everything she found, and since she read whole issues of medical journals, not just articles on subjects she'd already decided to write about, at least sometimes the information available seems to have helped her make up story.

The more you learn about ways of life that are unfamiliar, the easier it will be to imagine the kind of trouble and fun your characters might get into.

The editor of the quarry doesn't discuss *when* in the process of writing *Middlemarch* George Eliot wrote the quarry. It seems clear to me that she began writing the book before she wrote at least the second part of the quarry, which consists of list after list, like the ones I saw at the Houghton Library—plans for scene after scene. The lists refer to Dorothea from the first, and we know that Eliot wrote some of the Lydgate chapters before deciding to make her a character. So the second part of the quarry must have been written when she was no longer stuck. When she writes in her journal, "I have achieved little during the last week except reading on Medical subjects," maybe she's referring to the notes she took that make up the first part of the quarry—which would mean she began the entire quarry *after* she'd begun the book. She didn't write about Dorothea in her journal for more than a year after that. Perhaps she turned the quarry over to start again from the back at about the time she did the same thing with the journal, and then began planning the book as she now intended to write it—and did write it, including Dorothea.

Eliot began the second part by writing down information she'd acquired on other subjects besides medicine—political history, student life, and jobs in hospitals, much of which she didn't use. Then she writes the word "Middlemarch" in the middle of a page, and from then on, almost everything is about the novel. She lists the names and professions of minor characters. She draws a little map, just dots indicating the town of Middlemarch and the villages around it. The facsimile of the quarry on the Web makes clear that the author kept crossing things out, I think sometimes because she changed her mind and sometimes after she'd finished writing a section.

After the map she makes a list of "Relations to be developed"—Dorothea and Mr. Casaubon, Lydgate and Rosamond, and so on: who has to know whom. Maybe it served as a reminder to write scenes in which characters meet, so they'd have a relationship when the plot required one. If I had learned nothing else as a novelist from seeing the quarry, this list of relationships would have made it helpful.

Next we find a list of "Private dates"—the years when events in the book will happen. At first they're listed haphazardly; then she repeats part of the list, putting some events in chronological order and adding detail—and that method, listing and then repeating a list in more detail, becomes her habit all through the quarry. A series of lists: it's a way to keep things straight and yet to change your mind.

Most of the rest of the notebook consists of lists of scenes or chapters—phrases summarizing the contents of the eight books into which this novel is divided. As I noticed when I saw the original quarry, nearly all the chapter summaries describe actions: "Sir James appeals to the Rector" or "Featherstone asks for something awkward."

Eliot keeps changing her mind, and book 3 changes the most. Some scenes in the finished book are not in the same order as on the list. Other important scenes seem not to have occurred to her when she first compiled the list. They bring important relationships to life: it's in these scenes that Dorothea gets to know the man she will eventually love. Some scenes are shifted a third time—and in the actual book the order of these events is different yet again. Eliot is making a plan—but it's a fluid plan, a succession of plans, a plan that recognizes the intuitive, disorderly nature of the process she's engaged in.

After the plans for the third part, she comes up with something else, a list she calls "Motives," which are broadly defined movements, not yet divided into scenes: "Featherstone's burial. Arrival of Ladislaw." Next, the "motives" are divided into chapters. She continues that way, with lists of motives followed by lists of chapters. A few have question marks in front of them. She proceeds all the way through to the end of the novel.

Then she makes some general plans again, with a list of the ages of some characters. And then she does something she hasn't done before: she writes an account of one character's history: facts that are slowly revealed at the end of the book and make it suspenseful are worked out here as if in their own story. Then Eliot *again* makes lists for the middle and the end of the book. It feels as if she got to a point where she didn't feel completely at ease with the plan she had, so she redid it, again moving from the general to the more specific—as if she's thinking through the book over and over, telling herself the story, noting down what she's telling herself.

Book 6 is planned several times, with the lists of events becoming more and more specific. "Fred Vincy choosing his career" becomes "3. Fred Vincy has an adventure 4. In consequence seeks employment with Mr Garth." As before, what's in the quarry is what moves the story along.

What's in the *book* is a lively, spontaneous scene. Mr. Garth is a surveyor and property manager. He's practical, unpretentious, and scrupulous (goodness is tangible in George Eliot). Fred Vincy has been trained for the church, but is so unspiritual and restless with indoor life that the woman he loves—Mr. Garth's daughter—has told him she won't marry him if he becomes a clergyman. He can't figure out what else to do until this scene, where he comes upon Mr. Garth working. Nearby a bunch of ignorant farmers with pitchforks are attacking surveyors working on a new and terrifying phenomenon: the railway. Fred and Mr. Garth save the surveyors, and Mr. Garth scolds the farmers. When Mr. Garth's assistant sprains his ankle, Fred helps hold the measuring tape—and that's how he ultimately becomes Mr. Garth's assistant and leads a good life after all.

Eliot is coming to the end of her novel. After the list of scenes in the quarry, she writes, "How to End the Parts"—major events at the conclusion of each section—and then "Remaining Scenes of Part VI" and another summary of events.

For book 7, near the end, she becomes less orderly. She asks herself questions: "What becomes of Bulstrode's arrangements as to property, especially Stone Court?" She makes notes she doesn't fully explain: "About Dorothea's money, over and above her own 700 a year."

When she reaches the last part, book 8, it feels as if she's thinking aloud: "Reasons why Dorothea does not immediately have her interview with Lydgate." When she writes her usual numbered list of scenes, the numbers no longer refer to chapters. She's just enumerating events, apparently to help herself keep them straight as she writes.

The plan in George Eliot's quarry for *Middlemarch* feels familiar to me: it resembles the progress of a mind thinking, of my own mind and maybe yours, of the lists and more lists I write when I'm working on a novel—each the bones of a book, each different. When the lists are no longer helpful, they are superseded. Her process is not just to break something large into smaller parts, as an outline does, but to keep rethinking the larger divisions as well, reaching back and forth from large to small, but also from small to large.

The quarry's method is organic and fluid, and much easier than trying to figure out a whole book at once. It takes advantage of the way a mind moves through a thought: associating, getting ideas, coming to a new understanding, rejecting that understanding, trying another. And it does so about a huge intellectual project. It uses a mixture of rational and irrational thinking: logical progress interrupted when the needs of storytelling or the nature of the characters make the plan wrong. I think it's a quarry in part because it contains material Eliot could use when she wanted it, and in part because she's making a mess in order to make something orderly. She's excavating rough ground here. Like people setting out to cut building blocks from a hill of rock, she can't say in advance exactly what she'll find or from what angle she'll approach it, to get the right piece out of the quarry and into words. Thinking hard, not taking her thoughts too seriously, and thinking again helps her write a book that feels alive and unpredictable on every page. It's not the only way to write a novel, but it's one way.

CHAPTER 7

What Killed the Queen? and Other Uncertainties That Keep a Reader Reading

It's Long Enough to Be a Novel, but Is It a Novel?

Like (I am told) long-distance sailing and hiking the Appalachian Trail, writing a novel is a difficult experience that is supposed to be fun. George Eliot wrote *Middlemarch* despite sickness and sorrow and, as we've seen, a more workaday problem when she began: not yet having a story that felt right. She got unstuck after she researched the period she was writing about and combined two ideas that she hadn't considered using together.

Then she wrote a great novel. The story—Lydgate, Dorothea, Bulstrode, Casaubon, Will Ladislaw, all that—is compelling, moving, and meaningful. But what if, however you go about it, you complete a manuscript that looks at first glance like a novel but isn't *exactly* a novel, and nobody wants to read it—maybe not even you? It's just—sorry—too easy to put down.

Eliot listed the parts of her novel, as we've noted, according to the action that would occur in them. I don't mean that her book is full of action—it isn't. But thinking of what happens in a novel as a series of acts that lead to other acts—whether vigorous or quiet—is useful, and difficult for many new writers. People I meet often assume that after they invent a character, their next job is to choose that person's central, deepest need or conflict or psychological hang-up, then make up experiences that took place before the time of the novel, to show how he or she came to have that trait. A character who is afraid of intimacy had neglectful parents; someone who is angry was mistreated. Some students in writing classes have been told to make up stories about a character's past, and what they come up with is often a psychological history about formative childhood experiences.

When that character then appears in a story or novel, the author primarily has in mind major personality traits arising from childhood, and if I ask the writer, "What will happen in the next scene?" the answer is something like "I will demonstrate Gregory's insecurity about ___ and his fear of ___." However interesting it may be to think of characters as—in part—the results of their personal history, focusing too intently on psychology makes writers look back, not forward.

I too like complicated characters. I too am more interested in character than in a suspenseful plot. But the expression of psychological complexity through—primarily—a series of actions is what makes fiction work. Characters do things.

I suspect that when writing instructors suggest that new writers make up stories about their characters' earlier lives, they are hoping not for accounts that will simplify matters by explaining behavior, but for past events that may complicate the *story*, offering suggestions for event. After all, for a short story and even more for a novel, we need plenty of enterprise and uncertainty. If you invent a history, make it one that will suggest not character traits but situations and actions. What might someone *do*—someone, that is, who as a result of her history has, say, little money but a boat she's inherited, or a cleaning woman she can't pay, or responsibility for a troubled nephew?

You'll think about her personality too, of course. You'll make decisions about what she's like, what's hard or easy for her, what moves her or fails to, and maybe what happened to her in the past. Her personality and history will matter at every juncture. But there will be junctures—happenings. You won't make your story a *demonstration* of her personality. It's fine for a writer to think a great deal about character. Problems occur when she thinks all but exclusively about character: then there's no particular reason for the next scene to come next.

When a reader (including the author) keeps looking for excuses to stop reading a novel, the book often turns out to consist of incident after incident written in no particular order, each often quite interesting and psychologically revealing, but with nothing in one incident to make the reader want to see what comes of it in the next. Episodes may be interesting, but we don't know why they are there. Books may jump around in time for no reason, nor does the reader have any confidence that they'll ever stop jumping around in time. Many pages from the beginning, we still don't know where the story is going.

Writing whatever comes to mind without planning, I know, isn't a bad way to begin a first draft, and we occasionally hear that fine books began just that way. We don't write well without touching on painful subjects, and many of us need to write for a long time before those painful thoughts emerge from wherever we ordinarily hide them. Writing without a plan, we make discoveries. And then, with luck, a compelling story forms itself under our typing fingers.

But what if we don't have that luck? The authors of the unfinished books I am talking about don't know what to do if they never receive an inspirational flash that makes their pages behave like a novel. Also, in writing—sometimes for hundreds of pages—without direction, and thinking almost exclusively about character and the feel of individual moments, these beginning novelists run out of material. When we write a scene on page 200, we use what we may have known all along about a character's quirks and passions, but we know what he or she is *doing* because what's happening is partly a consequence of events on pages 100, 150, and 180. Part of the purpose of action is to suggest to the writer another event later. If early in the book someone announces a deadline, then later the deadline must be met or, with consequences, not met.

A problem is or isn't solved. A confusion is cleared up or made worse. Would-be novelists with a heap of pages need to know how to stop, decide where the novel is going—what's the most important action?—and impose some kind of structure on what is there, however loose: to organize the events that are already written down—or think up new ones—so they keep a reader involved.

The Death of the Queen

Whatever else we want from a novel, we require *some* sense of a direction, even if parts seem to come out of nowhere when we read them for the first time. Something enables us to distinguish between forward motion and digression. We think of a novel as moving from beginning to end, not end to beginning. We think of it as a road, not a meadow, though it may have a proliferation of side stories, digressions, and descriptions—detours, alternate routes, and rest stops—within it. It is different from a collection of connected stories, which may be thought of as a group of routes that intersect, like the New York City subway system, or that take off from a center, like the T in Boston. Stories can usually be read out of order, but you'd better not start reading a novel with Chapter 5. Can we agree that readers of a novel (maybe leaving aside some experimental fiction) require something to persuade them to read in a direction and to keep reading, instead of picking the book up, reading at random here and there, and stopping in the middle?

Most often, the parts of a novel lead us along because the first event causes the second event, and so forth. And when we start thinking about an event leading to another event, we are thinking about plot. It's hard for most of us to say exactly what a plot is, and even before we start inventing one, we begin worrying that it will be too neat, too contrived—phony, like the silly, unlikely plot in a bad movie. Yet, as we've noted before, a plot can be quite simple, just enough to keep us involved. Almost all I remember of a college creative writing class is what the professor said about rabbits: a novelist starts up a certain number of unanswered questions as hunters might release rabbits they hope to hunt down in the course of the day. Too many rabbits and they can't shoot them all before dark; too few rabbits and they're done at lunchtime. Same with novels. It's a brutal but possibly a helpful simile.

The lectures E. M. Forster gave at Trinity College, Cambridge, in 1927, published as *Aspects of the Novel*, include the best description I know of plot (and story—Forster makes a distinction between them). He says story is just an event followed by another event, moving through time, and it provides the most basic kind of narrative entertainment: a series of exciting moments, so the reader or audience simply waits for the next one. Stories that are nothing but event after event (like Scheherazade's) must pause at unresolved moments for suspense. A novel with no plot, only story, manages, I guess, by inserting a mention of the next adventure before the end of the last one ("But just as the wolf slunk away, Lionel noticed a wisp of smoke. . . .").

A plot, Forster says, is something more. It appeals to memory and intelligence as well as to the capacity to be scared and shocked: the reader keeps in mind what has come before and thinks about it to understand what comes later. He writes:

> We have defined a story as a narrative of events arranged in their time-sequence. A plot is also a narrative of events, the emphasis falling on causality. "The king died and then the queen died" is a story. "The king died, and then the queen died of grief" is a plot.

For a long time I puzzled over this king and queen, because "The king died, and then the queen died of grief" *couldn't* be the plot of a story or novel. For the king's death to be a plot event, in Forster's terms, we'd need to be curious about what it would do to the queen. But Forster doesn't mean it's organized as a plot, only that it contains what a plot requires.

He goes on to say, "Or again: 'The queen died, no one knew why, until it was discovered that it was through grief at the death of the king.' This is a plot with a mystery in it, a form capable of high development." Later he says that "mystery is essential" to a plot, and surely he is right, even though mysteries in fiction needn't be hair-raising, as long as we are made to wonder, even if it's only, Will these unhappy people take this opportunity to make a difference?

"The queen died, no one knew why" sets a plot in motion, because the people around the queen are mystified from the beginning—and the presence of the plot is also what gives the story forward movement: we start with the death of the queen and keep reading to find out what killed her. The novel might begin with her sickness and then look back at the past as a detective story does, with the detective trying to figure out what happened before she came along. Or, if the novel began with the death of the king, somebody might say, early on, "I'm worried about what this will do to the queen."

Similarly, a hurricane followed by an election is a story—an event, another event—but if the government's response to the hurricane affects a coming election, then we have a potential plot, especially if the people caught in the storm start talking about the inadequate governmental response while the water is still lapping at their feet, or if the narrator hints about what's coming.

Some of the shapeless novels-in-progress I've seen in years of teaching have taken the form "The king died, and the queen died of grief," but lacked that hint. I might read a long account of the death of the king, but I didn't know why I was reading it until the queen finally got around to her annual physical on page 110. A plot worthy of the name needs to push us forward, if only subtly, not just to be worth reading in retrospect. Chekhov said that if a gun is mentioned in the first act, it must go off by the third. And it stands to reason that if the shooting of the gun is to be an effective plot element in the third act, the gun probably should be mentioned in the first.

Can we say then that a plot is a series of events arranged in a way to arouse enough curiosity to carry us through a story? Except that events aren't the only sources of curiosity, and even meandering, messy stories can take on just enough direction to keep us going. In the remainder of this chapter, we'll look at examples of whatever makes us curious, whatever provides forward momentum—acknowledging that dramatic events that cause other events to happen—or compelling but quiet events that also lead to other events—are the customary way of keeping us involved. Other ways include form that tantalizes us with the promise of repetition, variation, and resolution; partial revelation of what's coming (hints and foreshadowing); and signals of emotional shifts, like "She began to feel uneasy" or "She changed her mind: she would try to stop him." Sentences like those may have the same use in a book as an elaborate structure of action, coincidence, chance, and vengeance. What makes us feel anticipation may be any of these.

Whatever it is, its placement matters. When I speak of what makes us curious, I assume that the writer is aware of the reader, at least dimly, and that deciding what to write next—what sentence or what scene—partly has to do with keeping the reader curious—informed but curious.

As we read a good novel—or any narrative—we can identify sentences, bits of dialogue, or events that keep us interested, and as we revise our own drafts we can often supply something comparable. Simple reminders that somebody is in charge—that somewhere there's an author, and that the author, at least, thinks we're moving in a direction—may give us all the reassurance we need to keep paying attention. When a friend tells us a story, a sentence like "Bear with me, I'm telling you this for a reason" can make us willing to sit through a long digression. Words like "But to understand why the day was a disaster, you need to know something about my brother's past" can transform what may seem like random information into something that feels purposeful, and unless we have learned that this particular storyteller promises more than she delivers, such a sentence makes us trust her. Like Wallace Stevens's jar in Tennessee that "made the slovenly wilderness / Surround that hill," the unremarkable statement transforms the rest of what's there into something no longer haphazard.

But first of all—or maybe not first but eventually and most

importantly—the novelist needs that big issue, the unfinished business that will carry a reader along for many pages, and this discussion of novels assumes that if you are writing a novel, you have one in mind. You may need to think up subordinate questions as well, but you certainly need that main one, and if you are writing a novel but still don't have it, it might be a good idea to stop and figure out what it is. If your book is about a family, think of your story not as a portrait but as a *chronicle*—an account moving through time—about how a family changes, how it becomes rich or poor, how it gives up its integrity or restores it, how it deals with trouble or fails to, or how one person in the family saves herself, or doesn't. If the book is about a trip, make it a quest. If it's about conflict, make the conflict lead to someone we care about losing or winning.

The Wide, Straight Road

Herman Melville's *Moby-Dick* was published in 1851. Everyone remembers the central story. A man who tells us to call him Ishmael signs up as a sailor on a whaling voyage departing from New Bedford, Massachusetts. The one-legged captain is obsessed with finding and killing a white whale, Moby Dick, who tore off his leg in a battle. Most of the crew become equally invested in this quest, and the ship, the *Pequod*, travels for several years until it meets Moby Dick, who destroys the ship and everyone in it except Ishmael. I first read *Moby-Dick* many years ago, and when I began rereading it recently, I assumed there would be several subplots I had forgotten, but no, this book asks one question near the beginning—Where the hell is that whale?—and churns forward for hundreds of pages until the question is answered. A diagram of the story would consist of a single road prominently posted with ONE WAY signs.

Of course, there is more to it than that, and much more to all the novels I'll discuss than whatever makes us curious. We may be as curious as can be, but if the writing is trite and the characters aren't psychologically complex and believable, if the events are implausible—if the author has lied about the way things work in the real world, or has made characters do what these people, given what we know about them, would not do—then a book may be fun momentarily, but it's finally unsatisfying. What makes a novel good or great is usually not what keeps the reader curious; it's just that without something to make the reader curious, a novel isn't a novel. A cardboard container has little value by itself, but without it a cup of coffee is a puddle on the floor.

Ishmael is an engaging character who talks directly to the reader and goes into much more lively, passionate detail than would be necessary simply to tell the story. Here he is, near the beginning, explaining why he went on a whaling voyage. Melville awakens our curiosity by describing Ishmael's curiosity:

> With other men, perhaps, such things would not have been inducements; but as for me, I am tormented with an everlasting itch for things remote. I love to sail forbidden seas, and land on barbarous coasts. Not ignoring what is good, I am quick to perceive a horror, and could still be social with it—would they let me— since it is but well to be on friendly terms with all the inmates of the place one lodges in.

Part of what's appealing about *Moby-Dick* is Ishmael's friendly but elevated, self-involved, slightly quirky narration. Then there's our sense that the whale is more than a whale. The story is as much about evil and the frightening human wish to approach it—the lure of the forbidden—as it is about whaling and the sea. The feeling that everything in the book matters in at least two ways makes it exciting to read even when the story sags.

The story does sag. It's full of digressions about whaling and whales, quirky essays on such topics as "The Sperm Whale's Head" and "The Right Whale's Head," which seem charming to some readers and tedious to others. Overriding each interruption, always remaining in our minds, to be sure, is the unrelenting question of the book—Where's the whale, where's the whale? But the digressions don't move the story along, and some people skip them. If the book as a whole is a wide, straight road, the digressions are cul de sacs, and like the UPS driver who must turn down each of these dead ends, as a reader you may keep in your mind the speed and movement of the road itself, but as often as not you aren't on it. The novel does not have subplots—secondary chains of events—but it does have self-contained dramas that are compelling in their own right: the occasions when the *Pequod* encounters a whale that's not Moby Dick, or another ship. Some of the officers and crew have personalities and passions of their own, and we come to care about them, but their actions don't alter the main action of the book: the obsessive movement toward the white whale. In other words, this book has a story, in Forster's terms, but not really a plot.

Not many novels—except maybe detective stories—have a source of forward momentum that's as clearly stated and simple as *Moby-Dick*, and unlike a detective story, the account of looking for the whale doesn't have much intricacy—there are no false sightings, frustrating delays, or clues that come to nothing. If it didn't offer more than its simple story, it wouldn't be very good. What makes it great is the convincing horror of Ahab's obsession, the boldness of the novel's reach and its intensity, the richness of its descriptions, and the way details about the whale and the sea suggest at all times something even larger than the sea. Melville doesn't say what that larger thing is or moralize about it, and his reticence makes the whale a symbol more effective than most, as mysterious and powerful as it's supposed to be. At the end, when Ishmael quotes the book of Job—"and I only am escaped alone to tell thee"—the implied claim that Melville is writing about events that are beyond ordinary experience feels justified.

This is an adventure story—a story about one interesting episode after another, the most exciting coming last. If your novel falls easily into that form, you can simply tell what happened, as Melville did—say, if your story too is the story of a search with one goal and a series of gripping events along the way. You'll need a dramatic ending, but I suppose you know what that is already. But because this form is all but plotless, the story must be extremely compelling, the writing extremely good, to make the form work.

The Scenic Route

We've considered George Eliot's *Middlemarch* as an author's project—but how does it work for the reader? *Middlemarch* has not just one big issue that concerns us all through the book, but a series of separate stories within the larger story, each of which creates its own suspense: by the time one is resolved, another has captured our interest. If reading *Moby-Dick* is like driving on the interstate from New York to San Francisco, reading *Middlemarch* and other novels of its kind is more like driving to the West Coast with a pause to see a cousin in Pittsburgh, who says, "You should stop at the Art Institute of Chicago." When you do, you decide to devote your life to the paintings of Edward Hopper, and you also run into a college friend who invites you to go hiking with him in the Rockies. There you get lost, and the volunteer rescue party that finally turns up includes a brilliant art history professor, who will end up directing your dissertation on Hopper. And so on: separate but linked enterprises keep us involved, each for many pages, and there's always another one by the time the first is resolved.

Such a book may work with far less action than *Middlemarch* has. Thomas Mann's *The Magic Mountain* recounts in relentless detail the story of Hans Castorp's sojourn at a tuberculosis sanatorium in the Alps, first as a visitor, then as a patient: he comes for three weeks—which are narrated hour by hour over more than two hundred pages—and he stays for seven years. One of Mann's preoccupations is time, how quickly months and years pass when nothing is going on, and how—as he demonstrates—it changes shape, so a year or an hour can take the same number of words to narrate. Mann plays with this idea until the reader is as curious about how he'll break up and stretch out time as about anything else. The book tells a story in which, in large terms, nothing happens: Hans Castorp is removed from life, and does almost nothing but eat (they eat five meals a day in the sanatorium), take walks, and lie on a chair on his balcony, wrapped in blankets when it's cold, as it usually is. But in this slow, solemn recitation, the events that do occur become as exciting as more dramatic ones in a different book (and the book eventually includes an episode in which Hans Castorp is lost on skis in the snow, a duel, and a couple of suicides). Though the novel often amounts to an exposition of ideas, with power deriving from the characters' fierce disagreements, Mann also uses devices that any novelist might use to hold the reader's attention.

Throughout the first quarter of the book, we guess that Castorp will be diagnosed as tubercular, becoming a patient instead of a visitor, and we wait with growing anticipation for him to discover that, by the standards of the doctors in this place (who think every-one is sick), he too is sick. When he finally takes his temperature, the seven minutes in which he keeps the thermometer in his mouth are acutely suspenseful. By the time he is diagnosed, he's in love with one of the patients, and we wait for them to look at each other, pass each other in a corridor, and—eventually—speak. She leaves, after they have spent one night as lovers, but now there are other issues—and eventually she comes back.

The Magic Mountain is what's called a novel of ideas, but whether a character will understand an idea can be as suspenseful as anything else, and much of this book consists of Hans Castorp listening to an Italian humanist and an authoritarian Jesuit argue about the spirit and the body—life and death. Foolish Hans Castorp insists that both men are equally interesting, and the reader frets over him. The sanatorium, we come to feel, represents death, and so does the Jesuit, who denies that human life has value. We become desperate to know whether Castorp will see what is clear to us: that one of these men is right and the other is wrong.

Each uncertainty, again, keeps us interested, at least until we reach the next. When the woman Hans Castorp loves comes back, she's accompanied by a fool named Peeperkorn. Hans Castorp is even more enthralled with him (though he and Peeperkorn are rivals for the woman) than with the humanist and the man of God who have been struggling for his attention. Then, writing of Peeperkorn, the narrator mentions "the end of his stay," and the narrative continues with a supposed discussion between author and reader:

—The end of his stay? So he did not stay on longer than that?—No, no longer.—So he departed?—Yes and no.—Yes and no? No mystery-mongering, please. Surely it can be said straight out. . . . And so our vague

Peeperkorn was carried off by his malignant tropical fever, is that it?—No, that's not what happened to him. But why this impatience? Not everything can be known right off. That must still be taken as one of the conditions of life and of storytelling, and surely no one is about to rebel against God-given forms of human understanding.

Along with these uncertainties, Mann's psychological insight gives each incident vitality and interest. Also, like novels about universities, boarding schools, ships, or artists' colonies, this is a book about a microcosm. The sanatorium suggests a world, a world so in love with death that no one in it can move—until, at the end of the book, the First World War begins and shocks the patients back into life.

An Elevated Highway

Sometimes a plot stays in the reader's mind all the way through, even though the book includes much that's not directly connected to the plot. Hemingway's first novel, *The Sun Also Rises*, has a more developed plot than *Moby-Dick* or *The Magic Mountain*, but the plot takes up few words. Like those books and like *Middlemarch*, this one includes incidents that move the story along and long stretches that don't, but this book is organized differently. The characters are American and English expatriates living in Paris after the First World War. It's a perfect tourist's novel, because the neighborhoods and landmarks where the characters drink and run into one another are familiar if you've ever spent even a couple of days in Paris. After a while it moves to a fishing trip in the mountains, then the bullfighting festival in Pamplona. Much of the story could almost be a travel diary, but it's shaped around a suspenseful sequence of events that lead to other events, events that embody the conflicts within the characters' personalities. Instead of just wandering around drinking, watching bulls die, and feeling alienated, they take action—or refrain from action—in a way that turns their feelings and wishes into a story. Nearly all of each scene is just an account of a place and its pleasures, but every scene has a reason for being in the book, because each one includes a few paragraphs in which a remark or event or question turns the drinking and bullfighting into background.

Jake Barnes, as everyone knows, was wounded during the war and is impotent, which in Hemingway's scheme of things is not mere "erectile dysfunction" but a tragedy. Jake loves a British woman, Lady Brett Ashley, who plans to marry a man she doesn't love: she loves Jake Barnes, but she can't do without sex. Then a friend of Jake's also falls in love with Brett. Much of the plot has to do with the friend's efforts to woo her, as they all eventually meet up in Spain. Brett becomes infatuated with a bullfighter, who represents a kind of hope: his physical prowess, courage, and adherence to tradition suggest the possibility of a life with honor, which seems impossible to the disillusioned and wounded main characters. Near the end, Brett runs off with the bullfighter, but then calls upon Jake to come to her in Madrid. She has left her lover, and she and Jake return to Paris. They can't have what they want, but at least Brett has refrained from spoiling the bullfighter's life.

It seems that Hemingway began with experiences from his life—drinking, fishing, going to bullfights—and placed a plot on top of them, so that each scene is dominated by a question in the reader's mind. Say you wanted to write a novel but all you could think of was your own day: breakfast, work, lunch, child care, and so on. By superimposing a series of questions or uncertainties on the scenes, you could give them point and direction. As your toddler throws Cheerios on the floor at breakfast, your phone rings: a colleague is in the hospital. You then meet your firm's accountant on the commuter train; she says she needs some financial records you have. This request makes you anxious as you try to admire the scenery outside the train, and at work you realize that only your sick colleague can explain certain troubling disparities in the bookkeeping. Quickly, you hide the documents behind the radiator. You have an extended, delicious lunch with your boss, who mentions over crème brûlée that the sick person has been rushed to surgery. Late that afternoon, you and your child are at the playground when a call comes. . . .

As in Hemingway's book, most of your pages are about your day, but the superimposed crises—even though each part takes only a few words to narrate—change your activities from foreground to background, and lunch is suddenly not part of a foodie's diary but a shrewdly understated, suspenseful scene, in which the only thing that matters, the crucial thing, is barely mentioned. Writing a novel like this will require you to invent a series of events causing other events, but if those events are sufficiently worthy of attention, you can also include many pages of ordinary life. Most narratives have long scenes in which nothing much happens except a dinner party or a car ride—but somewhere in those pages comes a discovery, the start of a mystery or a surprise—through a chance meeting, a phone call, an unexpected text message, a detour, an unguarded moment. The plot in this kind of novel is an elevated highway over a neighborhood, or maybe the monorail that crosses the Bronx Zoo, from which you can look down on the animals. The animals meander in their enclosures, but the train moves in only one direction.

Switchbacks

Writers I teach revel in making novels and stories jump around chronologically. I think they do this partly to show off—*they* can keep everything straight even if I can't—and partly to give readers so much to do, jumping around and sorting things out, that, the writers hope, no one will notice that the book has little going on in it: the suspense has to do not with what happens but with when the author will reveal something the characters have known all along. To be fair, I think these writers also violate chronology for a better reason: because thought is not chronological. In real life you think of lunch with your sister yesterday, then her eighth birthday party, then her wedding, and then what happened yesterday before lunch, and these writers have the legitimate wish for their books to seem lifelike. Violating chronology seems cool and sophisticated and sexy—and easy, since your mind too comes up with incidents out of order. It would be boring, these writers conclude, to work out a series of chronological events and plod through them like some dodo.

I disagree. Chronological order (interrupted, perhaps, by well-placed incidents from the past) is usually best, despite all this, just because it's clearest, and because it allows us to wonder what will happen next, as we do in life. Think of the last time you waited for the phone to ring—for the call from the people who'd found your dog, the doctor who had the test results, the angry lover. Breaking chronology not only gives away the ending but is distracting. It makes the reader think of the writer, not of the story. It's usually preferable to think about who did what than how clever this author is.

Or maybe not. Jumps in time may do more than imitate random thinking; they may do so artfully, so the process of thought has its own sequence of mysteries and revelations, as in *Mrs. Dalloway* or *Ulysses*. Or jumps may be undertaken in order to conceal and reveal information at just the right moments. Then, breaking chronology can make for a thrilling plot.

I mentioned Zoë Heller's novel *What Was She Thinking?* as an example of a book about the work of a teacher. It's also structurally interesting, and it's not in chronological order. The book is narrated by the older teacher, Barbara, who gives us two intertwining accounts, each chronological. The book is about an affair that the younger teacher, Sheba, has with a student, and its consequences. At the beginning of the novel—more than a year after the two women have met—we learn that Barbara and Sheba are living together, and we don't know how that came to be. Barbara begins her narrative with what's happening as she writes, then tells us the story of the past, starting when Sheba, then living with her husband and two children, came to teach at the school where Barbara has taught for many years. At times Barbara jumps ahead of her story to tell us what has just taken place, as she is writing. We could describe *What Was She Thinking?*—in which the forward motion in the reader's mind is achieved by forward motion along two separate time lines by the author—as a trail up a mountain, consisting of a series of switchbacks, so you are sometimes heading one way and sometimes the other, yet always moving closer to the peak.

Further complicating the structure, Barbara's account of the past itself consists of two narratives: first, her history with Sheba—how they met, what she thought of Sheba as time passed, and how she learned about Sheba's affair—and, second, what was really (as she now knows) going on with Sheba that she didn't know at the time.

It's not confusing, I think because the breaks in chronology resemble those that occur naturally in speech. "I'm having lunch with my boyfriend, Steve," says the friend you meet on the steps of a restaurant. "Yeah, Angus moved out six months ago—turns out he'd been otherwise occupied for a long time. Oh—there's Steve. Come say hi." Heller's three strands enable her to tell two stories at once: the story of the affair and, what gradually becomes even more important, the story of Barbara and Sheba's relationship. Heller's method here, using apparently random interruptions, lets her control the reader's growing awareness of Barbara's motives and personality—which turn out to be the real subject of the novel. Barbara seems to be a neutral informant and turns out to be the main character, with as much of a stake in the action as anyone. For example, one scene begins, "Just after I wrote that last sentence, Sheba rang me from the Beckwiths' shouting unintelligible things about Richard and asking me to come and help her." Barbara rushes over and actively participates in sorting out relations between Sheba and her estranged husband, making matters worse. The effect would be different if that scene came earlier or later. Because of the structure, Heller can put it anywhere she likes without our feeling that we're being manipulated by an author who refuses to let the narrator tell us what she knows. When writing a book that's not in chronological order, you can devise a schedule of revelations and dole them out one by one. It's a fine way to write a novel—but its advantage is primarily that it enables the author to control revelation. Violating chronology merely in order to imitate the wanderings of thought often doesn't provide enough benefit to justify what you give up: clarity and forward momentum.

Violating chronology works here also because the end of the story—which we learn first—is sufficiently complicated that we can learn something at the start (the two women live together) without learning everything (how on earth did *that* come to be?).

Many novels begin with characters in their old age, and then start over and explain how they got to where they are. That method works when the ending that's revealed in the opening chapter isn't the only source of suspense, and when it's strange enough that the reader does wonder what might have led up to this outcome. Or, if the final event *isn't* the one on which the reader's attention can most fruitfully be fixed, starting with it gets it out of the way.

But if you write your book in some order other than the chronological, common sense will tell you that you need to take a few precautions. Unobtrusively keep the reader informed enough to understand events that happen out of order, even if the understanding will be incomplete at first. You can give us a summary of an event in a way that makes us long to know the details. At each jump, make clear in the first few words which time line we're in. Consider just how much bafflement your reader is likely to enjoy.

Scavenger Hunts with the Children

Novels about family life are most like the shapeless manuscripts by new writers that I see—and indeed, those student manuscripts are often about families. There are reasons for a little shapelessness. Life—especially family life—does not feel like a well-plotted novel. Often it's chaotic. Events happen without connection to other events. Or nothing seems to happen at all, yet suddenly children have grown into adults. Can a novel be organized and pointed enough to keep a reader involved, yet sufficiently haphazard to be faithful to what we know of life, especially life in a family over the course of years?

We'll consider one novel and a series of novels: *The Fountain*

Overflows, by Rebecca West, and Edward St. Aubyn's five novels about Patrick Melrose: *Never Mind*, *Bad News*, *Some Hope*, *Mother's Milk*, and *At Last*.

In family novels, not much may happen week by week, but passions are strong. There is suffering, and the overriding question is not, as in a novel about a trip, Will they get there? but, Will these children survive to adulthood with any semblance of happiness? Will they live or die, surrender to despair or have good lives? Often, the family is poor, or the adults are eccentric, or defeated by illness, drink, or obsession, or are neglectful or cruel. Or a family may suffer prejudice or injustice. History may intrude, if only subtly. To bring in my road metaphor one last time, these novels, which move forward, but slowly and with surprising zigzags, are something like scavenger hunts, in which kids scamper along on a series of quirky or educational errands (find a used bus transfer; find an oak leaf; find a red hat). The completion of each task leads on to the next, and the children move on with purpose, though to a passing stranger their darting about may seem haphazard. The plot may be subtle; only in retrospect may we realize that our curiosity was always engaged.

Trouble is embodied in events. If the family is poor, there is not just daily, unvarying deprivation but a crisis involving money: a promise of money to come, a potential loss of a job or house. If the problem is neglect, a child will get hurt or sick; the neglect will have consequences. If there isn't a ready plot arising from the initial situation, the novel will find a plot, because there will be a series of threats, promises, deadlines—and, simply, the passage of time. We wonder who will live or die, fall in love or out of it, thrive or fail, and enough time will pass that we find out. And there's something else: often the authors of these books seem to take pleasure in writing about the inevitable absurdity of family life, the silliness of its passions and rages, and so the resulting book is at least partly funny. Nobody writes a good family novel who is afraid to embrace the ridiculous. Taking self-destructive people too seriously (good family novels always include some self-destructive people) wears out the reader along with the characters.

Rebecca West's 1956 novel *The Fountain Overflows*, about a family in England at the turn of the twentieth century, remains entirely in the consciousness of one child, Rose Aubrey, over the course of years. The book begins, "There was such a long pause that I wondered whether my Mamma and my Papa were ever going to speak to each other again." The reader has already learned from this sentence that there is trouble. Soon we discover that the problem is Papa, an idealist who, with charming optimism, gambles their money away on unlikely investment schemes. The children love him dearly, his wife—driven wild by him—is still faithful and devoted, and the reader (who likes him too) always knows he is impossible, and that he may doom his family. The most clearly marked path in this book is toward financial ruin and the inevitable departure of Papa, whose irresponsibility finally carries him off, whereupon it turns out that Mrs. Aubrey has kept from him one valuable source of money, so she and the children do not starve. She blames herself for this deception, even as she takes advantage of it. Ambivalence is a flourishing plant in *The Fountain Overflows*.

This book has a plot in Forster's sense—events arising from the father's improvidence—and two subplots. West recounts incidents in a leisurely, descriptive way, but each causes the next one, until a resolution is reached and something momentous has occurred. This is a family of musicians: Rose, her twin sister, Mary, and their mother are pianists; the mother was a successful concert pianist before her marriage. Cordelia, the oldest sister, plays the violin, but she has neither precision nor a sense of music. Rose, Mary, and their mother must suffer Cordelia's playing, and their politeness and agony are funny and heartbreaking. Then—and here West devises an event that gives Cordelia's lack of talent embodiment in the practical world—an equally unmusical teacher befriends Cordelia and pushes her into a performing career: she plays for ignorant boors who think she's wonderful. We read on, hoping and fearing that Cordelia will discover that she really *can't* play the violin. This book is the best fiction I know about what it's like to watch bad art achieve success while good art (Rose's and Mary's piano playing) goes unrewarded.

The second subplot involves a murder. The mother of a school-mate of Rose's kills her husband. The Aubreys take in the mur-derer's pathetic sister to shield her from public scrutiny, as the murderer is captured, tried, and almost executed. Mr. Aubrey, a political journalist, champions the accused woman, not because he thinks she is innocent but because the trial is unfair. This story intertwines with the others, and combined, they form a novel that keeps us reading while never imposing too much orderliness or predictability on the chaos of life. We stay involved because of these braided stories, and no less because of the novel's lovable and unbearable characters, not to mention Rose's irrepressible impa-tience with the people around her. This novel also includes modest departures from realism: a poltergeist, and Rose Aubrey's capacity to know people's futures—which is not a plot element but an ethi-cal challenge. She can tell fortunes, but should she? It's a book that beguiles us page by page and paragraph by paragraph—and it also has forward momentum, though that's not what we love most about it.

Edward St. Aubyn's five-part series of novels about the life of a wealthy British man named Patrick Melrose from the time he is five until early middle age—which St. Aubyn has said is based on his life—carries to extremes all the characteristics of the family novel. The first three books—*Never Mind*, *Bad News*, and *Some Hope*—are short. They were published close together, two in 1992 and the third in 1994. *Mother's Milk* came out in 2005 (St. Aubyn wrote other books in between), *At Last* in 2012. Reading these books at once feels like reading one long novel.

They have even less plot than *The Fountain Overflows*. There's plenty of event, but little that leads to later action, except as happens in any life as time passes. The books are funny —with outrageous juxtapositions and absurdities—but the humor is so dark, it will not strike some people as humor at all; in the last book someone says that Patrick Melrose's father had a good sense of humor, and Patrick says he was not funny but cruel. What keeps the reader involved is the essential questions in any family novel—Will this child survive this family? Can he save himself?

At the start of the series Patrick is five and the Melrose family are staying in their house in France, which figures in most of the books. The father, David Melrose, is habitually sadistic for his own amusement. The mother, who drinks, is oblivious to the child's needs or troubles. There is so little foreshadowing, emphasis, or arrangement that when David, on a whim, beats and rapes his son, it almost feels as if the reader is alone in thinking this incident more significant than the others. The climax is not treated like a climax. Repetitions of key phrases as they recur in characters' minds create subtle emphasis, but the tone is deadpan: this happens; that happens. In the second book, *Bad News*, Patrick is grown and a drug addict; on the first page he gets the news that his father has died on a trip to New York, and Patrick flies to New York, takes drugs there, and claims his father's body. In *Some Hope*, the reader—who of course has not been able to forget the rape, and has been waiting for the characters to talk about it—is finally satisfied when Patrick, now off drugs, tells a friend about it. In this book, at last, commentary is allowed, by both the narrator and the characters. There are memories and flashbacks; characters comment on the past. At the end Patrick feels "his soul, which he could only characterize as the part of his mind that was not dominated by the need to talk, surging and writhing like a kite longing to be let go. Without thinking about it he picked up the dead branch at his feet and sent it spinning as far as he could into the dull grey eye of the lake."

In *Mother's Milk*, Patrick (now an alcoholic who abruptly stops drinking near the end of the book) is married and has two sons. He struggles with two mothers: his wife, Mary, is entirely devoted to their second son and no longer wants a sexual relationship, while his mother, always self-involved and oblivious to Patrick's needs and feelings, now has given the French house where he spent his childhood summers to a charlatan who directs a phony spiritual foundation. His mother can still get Patrick to do what she wants, including (he's a lawyer) take the official steps to bring about his own disinheritance. The book is held together by the series of requests she makes to her son, and the reader hopes, each time, that for once either she will think of his needs or he'll refuse her; so this family novel in which everybody is always the same only more so actually has a forward-moving story. Brilliant chapters are written from the viewpoint of the children, who are almost supernaturally aware.

At Last takes place after Patrick's mother has died, and is an account of her funeral and the party afterward, with flashbacks to many other incidents. The funeral is hilarious if you are amused by unbearable people, but at the end we feel health in Patrick—he

phones his now estranged wife; he wants to see the children—
at last.

In the Patrick Melrose books, little happens—but there is plenty
for the reader to be curious about. Like other books with little plot,
these depend on the intensity of the characters' feelings and suffering as time passes: time is what makes us curious, not because we
ask What happened *next*? as in a fast-paced thriller, but What will
become of him? Patrick marries and has children; a fellow drug
addict and friend of his remains his best friend and becomes a psychoanalyst; and so on. The large issues in Patrick's life— the deaths
of his parents, the loss of the house in France, the ups and downs
in his marriage and friendships, and primarily his ability to hold
things together and live without despair and addiction—provide
the framework that makes a reader pick these books up each day
until they are finished. But the Patrick Melrose books take the family novel, with its usual lack of tautness, to an extreme. On page
after page nothing much happens, and what keeps the reader going
in the short run is simply excellence: sharp detail, edgy dialogue,
the rhythm of life passing—the sort of thing that makes you decide
to buy a novel when you've read half a page and have found it
appealing without knowing anything about the story. In any novel
what keeps us engaged is a combination of well-made paragraphs
and pages, and a well-made story. The looser the structure, the
more slowly the book moves, the better those pages and paragraphs need to be.

How can you be faithful to the randomness of life while giving
your books the shapeliness of art? If you don't instinctively come
up with enough story, stop and think up actions that will be tangible results of the characters' feelings and personalities, and will

have further consequences in other actions (remembering that deadlines and money are good sources of events). Let the characters' mistakes cause tangible differences that must be dealt with, not just regret and arguments. Pay attention to the order of events: if you don't write in chronological order, make that a conscious choice rather than an inattentive habit. Write in chronological order unless there's a good reason not to, making clear what's going on when you do violate chronology. If your novel begins with the most exciting event and then drops back six months or a year to tell how it came to happen, consider starting six months or a year back in the first place (you can find another interesting event to begin with), so that when your exciting event occurs, it will happen to people we know and care about. Give your people not just characteristics but characteristic action, and then let that action have results that accumulate until something big—something worthy of a novel—occurs.

With a plan in mind—just a sketchy one, maybe just a list of the four or five most important moments the book will have—you may find it easier to write: you'll be writing toward something you know about. Maybe you don't know what will happen in the next fifty pages, but you know that by the end of those fifty, perhaps, someone will refuse something another character wants and depends on, or someone will have fallen in love, or someone new will have arrived. Knowing what's coming, you can invent scenes that move you toward it. You can write a novel (or a book-length memoir) in all sorts of ways—but you're best off thinking of it as a *book*, not a pile of pages, not just a history, not a look around, but a story moving forward in time that carries the reader with it.

PART IV

Choosing to Speak

CHAPTER 8

Silence and Storytelling

Stories Not Told

When I was a child, my mother's mother, who couldn't read or write, occasionally asked me to write a letter for her. I'd bring my lined paper with pictures of puppies or bunnies, and she'd dictate a message to one of her sisters. She seemed comfortable with this method of expression, and I didn't wonder why she was illiterate; for all I knew, grandmothers generally couldn't read or write. I know now that she hadn't been taught as a child in Eastern Europe because she was a girl, and when her children tried to teach her, it was somehow too late.

The memory of my grandmother's illiteracy breaks my heart, and perhaps because of her, writing—especially by women—seems blessed, lucky. It exists despite obstacles and efforts to prevent it. One way writing is prevented—in addition to the obvious ones, like culturally or legally enforced illiteracy, government censorship, or informal censorship by acquaintances and relatives—is self-censorship. Years of teaching, observing my friends, and observing myself have made me aware that women in particular sometimes censor their own writing—either by not writing at all or by nervously writing in a way that keeps the reader from finding out what they have to say. Though writing by men (especially men who belong to groups that have traditionally been silenced) must overcome obstacles as well, I suspect that self-censorship—feeling unable to write or speak—is a problem women have felt more often (and have written about; many female characters in books by women can't talk, can't write, can't explain). But in this chapter I'm writing primarily about women, mostly because the majority of my students are women, and what I have to say here came in response to their work.

The women I teach are literate, of course, and often have been encouraged to write. Whatever their circumstances, they have found the time and money to attend the program in which we meet. Yet—and here is where they differ from most men I've taught, and resemble my grandmother—they sometimes don't seem to believe they *ought* to write, as if writing were self-indulgent. It seems to me that when a female writer's mother gets sick, the woman thinks she should stop writing and go look after her mother. When a male writer's mother gets sick, he thinks he should work harder than ever, sell a story to the *New Yorker*, and earn money to buy medicine for his mother.

We know that writing *is* self-indulgent, at least at first. You aren't reading this book unless writing has given you pleasure at some point. When we begin, we can't know that we'll ever write something that others will want to read; all we know is that we like doing it. But if we're serious about writing (willing to work hard, revise, accept criticism, read widely), our goal, soon if not immediately, must be to write what readers will want to read: to give pleasure to others, not just ourselves. So the new writer must gamble—risking time, work, self-esteem, and money on the supposition that what she's doing isn't entirely selfish. We say, "I think

I can write something worth reading," and then put in years of work before we know for sure. That's true for anyone, entering any profession—but isn't it more true in the arts?

The confidence to proceed without guarantees of success isn't easy for anyone to come by, but it must be harder for women writers, given the continued disparities in the publication of work by men and women, as demonstrated every year by VIDA: Women in Literary Arts, whose Web site lets us know that men still publish far more often, and are taken more seriously. If you are a woman, whether your piece of writing remains unread because publishers consciously or unconsciously have discriminated against it, or because—affected by a long history of discrimination against women—you have censored yourself and neglected to write it, finish it, revise it sensibly, or send it out and keep sending it out repeatedly if it's rejected, the fact is that all too often nobody's reading it. This chapter is about learning to do your part insofar as you can: overcoming a lack of confidence so you can write.

It's not necessary to feel confident. I don't have much confidence myself. I've learned to manage by regarding my need to write as something about which I have no choice. Like my eye trouble and other aspects of my life that are not under my control, my need to write just happened, and I don't try to decide whether it's bad luck or good luck. When a draft looks terrible, I don't try to convince myself that it's actually good or even that someday it will be, only that it's my job to work on it whether it's good or not.

I can't bestow confidence on you, but whether you feel confident or not, you can choose to behave confidently—to write as if you felt confident. I've said before that writing requires specific as well as general courage: not just the courage to type words but the courage to inhabit a character, to let your characters make mistakes and suffer. In this chapter I'm writing about another sort of courage:

the courage to choose a form for your story and the sentences within it that allows it to be told. You may not have control over the lack of confidence that distresses so many of us, but you may be able to make objective choices that cause you to tell the story clearly whether you're worried about it or not. At least you can choose, instead of unconsciously closing off possibilities in advance.

As I've met more and more students who have trouble allowing themselves to write, I've noticed certain problems that come up again and again in the writing they produce. For a long time I didn't connect the feeling *about* writing to the problems *in* the writing. Then I began to wonder. Often I came upon problems that at first seemed minor, technical, peculiar to one person, easily fixed. But they proved hard to fix, as if they arose out of something deep. And when they were solved, a weak writer sometimes surprised me, becoming remarkably good. My students were making choices that might have made perfect sense in a different story— but not in the one they were writing. It began to feel as if anxiety was dictating sentences, or suppressing sentences.

Once I had a student who was doing poorly in our MFA program, writing very little, though everyone admired her sentences and paragraphs—she was obviously able. She wrote extremely short stories in which nothing happened. A character might be seen reacting to something unspecified, or a couple might be trying to relate to each other after some unidentified crisis. It was all so brief and subtle that it was barely there.

After I read a story she'd written and had no idea what it was about, I asked her to write down what had happened in the lives of the characters during the hours or days just before what she described in the story: to start the narrative earlier. Whereupon her story grew from three pages to seventeen, and turned out to be about an act of violence in the country where she had grown up. It was one of the best stories I've ever read—no, I'm not exaggerating—and this woman went on to write brilliant story after brilliant story, all about her homeland. All I did was to let her know that I was interested in more than the tiny scrap of writing she'd already produced. She didn't have to think up events—she already knew what they were, but she'd lacked the confidence to write them down. She was easy to help, at least in those months we worked together, and had some dazzling success with stories she wrote then and shortly after graduation; she published, won a prize, was sought after by an agent.

Unfortunately, now that she's been out of our program for some years, managing without its structure and demands, and—as so many of us are—responsible for solving some serious family problems, this woman has stopped writing (though it seems to me she could take a few hours for her writing every week and harm no one). I shouldn't be naïve about the difficulty of resisting self-censorship. If it's as difficult for you as it is for her to write, you may always need to be in a class or group of some kind, to have somebody demanding writing from you, counterbalancing the voices—your own or other people's—that are telling you to keep your mouth shut. You may even have to struggle to convince yourself that it's all right to join such a class or group. Sometimes friends solve this problem for each other, setting deadlines and promising to write something by the deadline, then meeting in person or electronically to discuss it.

Ordinarily, when working with students who seem to be keeping themselves from telling a story, I see more complete stories than that student first submitted, stories with characters and situations, maybe several incidents. But a few difficulties come up again and again. As I read these students' work, I'm often confused—I don't know who the people are or how they know one another or what they're doing. This at first seems like a problem barely worth mentioning—the writer just needs to *say* that the brother is a professional landscape gardener, so that's why he's in the sister's backyard pulling up bushes, and why she feels guilty for not paying him. An easy fix—surely the writer will notice the difficulty herself; there's no need for a teacher to bring it up. No, quite often she doesn't. Something in her doesn't want the reader to know that the brother is a professional landscape gardener—or thinks it's unseemly to say.

Sometimes writers whose stories confuse me are telling them indirectly, though direct telling might be preferable. These stories may lack unadorned, informative sentences stating the essential facts about the characters' lives. They turn on important mysteries (Why is this woman taking a trip? Who are they all talking about?) that the characters themselves all understand; it's just the reader who doesn't—just *me*! (After a while I begin making frantic scrawls in the margins, feeling as if the characters are enjoying a joke or a secret and leaving me out.) Often the paragraphs concern the characters' mental processes more than what happens: I'm finding out what someone imagined or remembered or felt *after* something happened. Sometimes chronology is so fragmented that I can't follow the story at all. Other times there's a different kind of opacity: the events make sense one by one and may even be told chronologically, but I don't know why they are in the same story, what the characters want, and why they do what they do. And occasionally a story departs from realism in a way that doesn't add anything.

I suspect that when I come upon several sources of confusion at once, when I am baffled most of the time, I am reading an author who hasn't yet taken responsibility for the work: she (or he—sometimes it's a he) doesn't *want* me to know what's going on, because as long as I am baffled, I can't judge the story. For all I know, it's brilliant and the problem is just that I am not too bright. You don't want to write only for geniuses; give the rest of us a break. Decades ago I was teaching a creative writing class in which someone handed in a poem that was totally incomprehensible to me as well as to the students. I argued that having no readers at all just wouldn't be satisfying—clarity isn't everything, but it matters. Meanwhile, one very sharp young woman had been staring and staring at the poem. Suddenly she looked up, blinking, and said, "Is it about the House of Representatives?" It was. OK. Nonetheless.

Direct and Indirect Narration

Say a story begins, "Classico looked at Yarley and wondered what to do" and you're on page 3 before you discover that Yarley is a dog. That's indirect narration, which is worth explaining, since I for one didn't know what an editor meant when he said I was telling my stories indirectly (I am aware of these lessons because I had to learn them). Direct writing implicitly acknowledges that the narrator has a story to tell, and briskly informs the reader of what's going on: "Classico Johnson took her chocolate Lab, Yarley, for a run in Central Park one afternoon in October." Indirect writing begins as if the story started before we arrived, and implies that we're some-how overhearing what's going on, figuring out from clues what is happening. "Classico read Katchenary's message again. Yes, she had understood it correctly. How would they manage? And what if Katchenary found out what had happened on the way to the pond?"

There is certainly something seductive about indirect narration. Many of us fell in love with books when we read stories that were told indirectly. We learned to be patient and look for clues, gradually being drawn in, as if we'd been allowed to move into the characters' houses. If we just hung around quietly, after a while we'd learn who Katchenary was (it's pronounced CATCH-enary), what message Classico received from her, and, especially, what happened on the way to the pond.

A narrator telling a story directly may say, "I saw a horse." An indirect story may say, "I saw *the* horse," as if this is a horse we already know about, as if there's a story that started before we came along, and the horse was in it, as if we're one of the privileged group that has met this horse. When a story begins with "She" rather than with a name, it's indirect—or at least it has begun indirectly; many stories start with an indirect paragraph or two and then give you some facts: "Katchenary was Classico's sister." Though you'll have to wait to find out what happened on the way to the pond, you'll probably learn quickly that the message says that she's coming for a visit, and that she isn't welcome because she criticizes everybody.

The problem is when there are more mysteries, piled on without a thought for the reader, than anyone can take in comfortably. Here is an indirect opening that I made up as a bad example—though it's not too different from some that I've seen:

> She watched him open the box—which he'd brought such a distance, and after such a visit—and wondered what she'd do with what was inside.

It's mysterious, but what is the source of the mystery here? Isn't it that we don't know who "he" and "she" are, how they are connected, what sort of box this is, or where these people are—in what country or state or century? What is the benefit of withholding this information, of revealing it slowly, as one might reveal a secret? This particular opening is situated so deep inside the character's consciousness that the author isn't allowing herself to tell us anything the character is not specifically thinking. Since the character knows who brought the box and what's in it and has no need to announce these facts to herself, we can't learn who he is and what he's brought her unless the author can figure out an excuse for the character to think about what she wants us to know, in which case we get something like

> She watched him open the box—which he'd brought such a distance, and after such a trip—and, remembering earlier gifts from *her brother* and how much she'd disliked them, wondered what she'd do with what was inside, recalling a time when she'd eaten a whole *grapefruit* as a child and had vowed never to touch one again.

Ah, her brother! grapefruit!

Here is a direct opening for the same story:

> Classico watched her brother Ungartino open a wooden crate of pink grapefruit he'd bought for her in Orlando, where he'd spent a difficult week on vacation with their sister Katchenary. Classico, in her tiny New York apartment, had no room for so many grapefruits, and not much interest in eating them.

This isn't great literature (though I'm fond of the names, which were the names of my granddaughter's various imaginary friends when she was three), but at least it doesn't rely on withholding information to get the reader interested. After all, Classico knows what sort of box this is, Ungartino (accent on the penultimate syllable) knows—why shouldn't the reader know? Isn't it, finally, a cheap trick to create mystery about something that would be obvious to anyone present in the room? And if readers don't know what's going on in the plain old physical world, how can they pay attention to the legitimate mysteries of literature: how people (and dogs) love and hate, why they do as they do, or whodunit?

The Informative Sentence

One of my colleagues says he became a writer when he finally understood the value of a simple informative sentence, something like "Her brother was a landscape gardener." I'm not sure why sentences like that are difficult to write, but they are, for many. People have told me sentences like that are boring—which is like thinking that "Yes" or "No" is boring if you hear it in answer to the question "Is State Street that way?" It's not boring if you want to know.

There's also the lurking "show, don't tell" fallacy: the belief that because creative writing teachers advocate showing rather than telling (which is nothing more than the observation that "Harry knocked over his beer on top of my burger" is more evocative than "Harry was clumsy"), it is somehow against the law to tell *anything*. Thus we get long-winded descriptions of a small child who can walk but lacks teeth, or the other way around, so a writer can avoid telling us how old the baby is. Fiction earns its keep by bringing people and places to life, sure—but not all day long, not in every damn sentence. I include this shyness about plain facts in this chapter because it seems to me the problem is not just that new writers don't know they should say the baby was thirteen months old and the brother was a landscape gardener; they don't *want* to, even when they do know. It's too much of a commitment. It's like being the person in the group who says, "How about pizza?—I know a place on State Street, three blocks that way." If you're one of the people who invariably waits for someone else to take responsibility for what may conceivably turn out to be a bad dinner, start getting over this annoying trait by taking responsibility for what may conceivably be a bad idea in a story.

We don't need to know every tiny thing about your characters, and certainly not at first. Use the simple informative sentence for the things we do need to know if we're to understand your story: the facts that will make clear what we're seeing and forestall confusion. If you begin with a long conversation between a man and a woman at a breakfast table, the reader will assume they are lovers or spouses. If in fact the woman is the man's husband's massage therapist, having a cup of coffee because her client hasn't woken up yet, say so.

Mysteries

We've discussed the mysteries that can be cleared up with a fact or two. Now let's think about those that shouldn't be cleared up— or not quite yet: the scary thing that happened on the way to the pond, for example, and will thrill the reader when it comes out in the last chapter. It's fine to make your story turn on a delayed revelation. Readers get irritated, though, when there's no payoff— the revelation is that there wasn't a problem in the first place, or that the problem has been solved in some anticlimactic way. Also, it's irritating when the revelation is delayed too long. The longer we need to wait to find it out, the juicier and more surprising it had better be. And last—and most important—it's irritating when the narrator has known the answer to the puzzle all along and the reader doesn't.

It's possible to bring off a story in which the narrator knows the secret all along, but it's not easy, and if you're writing that kind of story, do it carefully and consciously. If the narrator is befuddled in some way—avoiding for long periods the thought of what he or she knows—or is inarticulate, the reader can sometimes accept the omission. Withholding information can also work if the narrator frankly is *telling a story*—we know all along there's a story, so of course there's a secret that the storyteller knows. In other words, the narrator tells the story not just directly ("At the beginning of last summer, I was spending all my spare time training my dog, Yarley") but in the voice of an acknowledged storyteller, who tells you she's telling a story and tells you there's something she won't say, or won't say yet, like Mann in the quote I included from *The Magic Mountain*, or this: "Before I tell you why Ungartino came, and what he did when he arrived, I want you to understand how Yarley and I spent our mornings at the pond." If you take on sufficient authority, you can carry off almost anything.

So the main requirement for putting a mystery into a story is being aware of what you're doing. Sometimes writers get an idea that's not yet developed but that seems right. Maybe as you wrote the sentence about Ungartino coming, you didn't yet know yourself why he came and what he did. If your kite is flying freely, that first draft may contain all sorts of possibly great ideas that may or may not eventually prove worth keeping. But pretty soon it's a good idea to stop, go for a long walk, with or without Yarley, and figure out what the story is and how it will be better if certain information is withheld. This isn't the sort of thing that comes on its own without effort.

Once, I was teaching remedial writing at a community college, and, to my surprise, a student began writing a novel. I was impressed: at the time I'd written no fiction of my own, and most of my students were reluctant writers of anything. He turned in many pages, an account of a trip by space travelers who were flying into the sun. One day I mentioned to him that I was in great suspense about how his characters would manage to fly into the sun and out again, and he said he hadn't figured it out yet. Soon the pages stopped coming. It's best to figure out how to get your space travelers through and out of the sun before you promise that you'll do it, or at least before you take the promise past the first twenty or thirty pages.

Characters Who Think on the Page

New writers often sprinkle mental processes through their fiction. Ungartino "still remembered" this and "wondered" that; he "fantasized about" something else. The mention of the mental process slows and muffles the story, which is now about remembering, wondering, and fantasizing rather than about the matters that Ungartino remembered, wondered, and thought about—actualities in the tangible world. Narrative is itself, of course, the result of mental processes that include remembering, wondering, and fantasizing. There may be a temptation, because we writers are so delighted by the inner life, to make the inner life the story and to write about people who do what we love to do: remember, wonder, and fantasize. We've considered this problem before. But I think an important reason writers say, "Ungartino still remembered when he and his sister hiked up to the summit," may be that they lack the storyteller's confidence, narrative authority: they can't quite believe that if they want you to know about the hike to the summit, they can simply write, "One morning several years earlier, Ungartino and his sister hiked to the summit." If Ungartino is the character from whose viewpoint the story is being told, and if he's *forgotten* the hike, after all, then we can't hear about it, right? So it proves that he remembers it if you tell us about it. There's no need to make every event in the story pass through a character's consciousness. Words about thinking emphasize that Ungartino has mental processes, but as we know, what happened is generally more exciting than how his mind works, the fact that he tends to daydream.

Chronological Confusion

As we know, thought isn't chronological, though life, inevitably, is. We've discussed the benefits and problems in novels that violate chronology, but the topic is worth mentioning again here, because I think the impulse to violate chronology comes in part from a love of mental processes as opposed to the tangible world—the introvert's experience, not the extrovert's—and in part from the same nervousness we've been discussing: a fear of pinning things down, making a commitment, being too definite, being out there saying, Hey, you, I'm the writer and you're the reader—and here's what happened!

Recently I saw a short story by a brilliant student who was resistant to changing her work at all. Apparently it was so frightening for her to write in the first place, that revision—going back and actually thinking about it—was simply terrifying. In the first scene something happened that was told so tangentially, with so few facts and so much emphasis on the main character's feelings—guilt and revulsion—that I didn't know what was happening. Though it was the first scene one read, it happened last, and once you had read the whole story, that opening scene made sense: the woman was in a subway car in which a panhandler was working the crowd—and the man was her father. I was sure that making the reader wonder what was going on couldn't possibly be more effective than telling the story in order and making that big scene come last, where it belonged chronologically. I didn't see this story again, but I don't think I persuaded the writer. I think she was too scared of the marvelous thing she'd made.

Murky Motivation

I don't think writers need to worry much about motivation. People in real life do all kinds of things for all kinds of reasons. It can be more useful to concentrate on *how* Classico came to adopt her dog, Yarley, the stages that preceded the action rather than the reasons. She said she wouldn't, she suddenly did—what happened in between? Maybe her boss wrote a bad evaluation of her, or maybe her mother got sick or her brother Ungartino moved to Paris—or the boss promoted her, her mother was declared cancer-free, or Ungartino moved in down the block. You could make any of these work, but we need to feel Classico groping from moment to moment and suddenly knowing that, after all, she needs that puppy.

Now and then I see a story with murky motivation: the character goes to the store, and then she adopts a puppy, and then she quits her job, and I have no idea why—or, it's not exactly why; I guess I have no idea *who*. The writer hasn't entered into the character enough, lent the character enough of her own substance and feeling, to make me feel that all these actions belong to the same woman on the same day. This too is a problem of anxiety—maybe it happens because the writer has trouble letting herself feel what's going on in real life, or maybe it just happens in writing, and it's because she's somehow shy with her characters. At first glance a story like this—with few references to what life is like emotionally, moment by moment, for this character—may seem elegantly understated, pared down to the essence. Just make sure there's an essence before you start paring.

Unhelpful Departures from Realism

I'm not sure that including unhelpful departures from realism in fiction is a result of a lack of confidence, but it may be: authors who secretly feel they have little to say sometimes decide they must turn to the supernatural. If you're drawn to something other than straightforward realism, of course you should write it. It's when writers say, "Maybe I should try magical realism," rather than "I would love to make that horse talk" that I worry. It suggests the fear that a straightforward story about realistic people and animals will be boring. Would a talking horse help? Do whatever you do, if you choose to, because you love reading books that depart from the expected this way, and you find that what your imagination comes up with crosses ordinary boundaries. Then introduce what's different in a way that lets the reader know that this universe isn't precisely the one we know; if everything in your book is realistic until page 234, when a horse talks—and provides the solution to the plot—the reader will think either that you don't know much about horses or that you've cheated.

The Elliptical Style

So much for the problems caused by lack of confidence: the observation that new writers sometimes write mysteriously not for aesthetic reasons but to avoid saying what they have to say. Many of the problems I've just described—stories shortened, events left out, stories told indirectly—are characteristic of the elliptical style, a style that, used well, contributes to the power of some of our best writing. It's the style that tells by not telling: narrative technique that tells the story by *pretending* not to tell it, or that tells the story by *pretending* to tell it reluctantly. The elliptical author *pretends* she doesn't want to tell the story, but she most definitely wants to tell it. She *pretends* she's just barely hinting, but she's writing something that is clear—though the revelatory statement may be in a subordinate clause, just barely there—and will stun you. The elliptical style omits rather than includes, going further than simply using no unnecessary words, always a good practice. Elliptical poems or stories may be extremely short, or frequently interrupted by white space: speech is punctuated by silence. When elliptical stories are long, they are still, in some way, not quite told. The narrator may hint at something that's never fully explained, or postpone revealing something she's known all along. Or she may tell a story indirectly, taking advantage of the reader's pleasure in entering a scene unobtrusively, almost by accident. But she shrewdly includes precisely what is needed for the overheard, indirect narration to be clear. In the remainder of this chapter, let's take a look at a few examples of the elliptical style used effectively, or used when there's no alternative.

Silence for Safety

Would a writer who was really censored—censored by a government—use the elliptical style? I began to wonder, so I turned to the poet Anna Akhmatova, who belonged to an active writing and publishing community at the time of the Russian Revolution, in 1917. For many years after that, it was illegal to publish her work in Russia, where she lived all her life. She never went to prison, but her son spent many years locked up, and many writers she knew were imprisoned and executed, including her first husband. Akhmatova was also informally censored by family members. When she was seventeen, her father threatened to disown her because she wanted to be a poet. Later her second husband forbade her to write.

After years of silence Akhmatova wrote again, and after Stalin died, in 1953, some of her work was published, but it was censored and sometimes banned or destroyed after it was in print. She died in 1966; some of her poems were never published in Russia in her lifetime.

Akhmatova's early poems, about love and emotional life, were written at a time when it was possible to publish. Even here, the style is indirect, but the indirection is effective; it brings reader and writer closer together. As Nancy K. Anderson, who translated the poet's work, writes in the collection *The Word That Causes Death's Defeat*, "Akhmatova's lyrics plunge into the narrative without pausing to supply background . . . , thus creating an effect of unexpected intimacy, as if the reader had accidentally overheard a personal conversation or come across a page from the diary of a stranger." She's writing about a poem beginning "Under the dark veil . . . ," in which a man turns away from a woman for a reason she doesn't know. The last stanza is

> I gasped as I shouted: "It was a joke,
> All of it. Don't leave me, please, or I'll die!"
> He had such a calm cruel smile as he spoke:
> "It's windy out here. Go on back inside."

It's impossible to quarrel with the use of the elliptical style here, to imagine that we'd be better off as readers if we knew what the supposed joke was, whether these lovers are married or not, how long they've known each other. The reticence is under control. We know they are lovers. We don't wonder if they are boss and employee or brother and sister. And exact details give the poem immediacy and particularity. Ellipsis, here, is used in just the right way; the only caveat I'd bring up is that this style would work less well if the characters weren't lovers. A short story writer I met who'd worked with a teacher who encouraged the elliptical style told me it was a revelation to discover later that fiction could be made of other life situations besides romantic love. Love, of course, is a good subject. But there are other subjects. What if you *did* want to write about an employer and employee, or, as in one of my examples, a massage therapist and the husband of her client? You'd need to state some facts.

Akhmatova deliberately chose an elliptical style during the later decades of her life; it would have been foolhardy to write straight-forwardly. "Poem Without a Hero," the great work of the last decades of her life, is essentially in code, obscure on purpose. It's a difficult poem, and apparently her contemporaries couldn't understand it either. Akhmatova rewrote and added to the poem over many years, and in a later section she claims that her editor objected to the first part, saying,

> The reader gets lost—it's still not clear,
> When all is done, who are the lovers,
> Who did what with whom, and when, and why,
> Who got killed, and who remained alive.

She refuses to explain; obscurity had been forced upon her, but she has made it her own.

In a stanza that was omitted altogether for many years, she writes about being silenced, about a poem of hers whose "mouth is crammed full of dry earth."

The next stanza—also omitted for years—reads:

> They tortured: "Spill it, tell us what you know!"
> But not a single word or cry or moan
> Gave her enemy anything to use.
> Years add up to decades—and each brings
> Torments, prison, deaths—for me to sing
> Amid such horrors—that I cannot do.
>
> (trans. Nancy K. Anderson)

"Requiem"—another late poem—commemorates the hundreds of hours the poet spent waiting in line at a prison, a parcel in her arms for her son. If the parcel was accepted, it meant the prisoner was still alive and was still at that particular prison—there was no other way to find out. In a note, Akhmatova says that once, in the line, she was recognized, and a woman asked, "Can you describe *this*?" She said, "I can." She does describe what happened—the poem is oblique, but it's comprehensible and moving.

When Akhmatova wrote "Requiem," it couldn't be published or even written down. Akhmatova memorized it and taught it to friends, who also memorized it. Her friend Lidia Chukovskaya wrote about this process in a passage quoted in *The Word That Causes Death's Defeat*:

> Anna Andreevna, when visiting me, recited parts of "Requiem" also in a whisper, but at home in Fontanny House did not even dare to whisper it; suddenly, in mid-conversation, she would fall silent and, signalling to me with her eyes at the ceiling and walls, she would get a scrap of paper and a pencil; then she would loudly say something very mundane: "Would you like some tea?" or "You're very tanned," then she would cover the scrap in hurried handwriting and pass it to me. I would read the poems and, having memorized them, would hand them back to her in silence. "How early autumn came this year," Anna Andreevna would say loudly and, striking a match, would burn the paper over an ashtray.

We can't know how Akhmatova would have written if she'd been encouraged to write all her life by her family and her government. Surely the practical necessity for a compressed, reticent style shaped her poetic choices as much as her innate sense of rhythm or language. In addition, as Anderson points out, practical necessity became emotional necessity.

The Silenced Character

Like Akhmatova, many writers—I think especially women writers—take up the subject of the woman who is somehow prevented from speaking. In her novel *Academy Street*, published in the United States in 2015, the Irish writer Mary Costello creates a young girl who loses the ability to speak after her mother dies and something shocks her: it is as if she cannot speak because she has no one to tell. She finds herself able to speak again, months later, to the one person in her household she trusts. Eudora Welty's 1972 novel *The Optimist's Daughter* concerns a woman who, like her father, cannot bring herself to say what she feels. After the death of her blunt, outspoken, but sensitive mother, her father has married a crude woman whose only similarity to the dead mother is that she too says whatever is on her mind. In several novels by the Anglo-Irish writer Elizabeth Bowen, girls or women (again, often with dead mothers) are prevented from speaking; when someone does blurt something out, often a catastrophe results.

Many of these novels are written in the elliptical style. Eudora Welty, for example, begins her book in the middle of something, and for a while you don't quite know what's going on. The first sentence of *The Optimist's Daughter* is indirect: "A nurse held the door open for them." The pronoun "them" has no antecedent, and for a moment we don't know who is passing through the door. Still, "a nurse" tells us something. She's not called "a young woman in a uniform" to add mystery. And the second sentence tells us straightforwardly who and where the characters are: "Judge McKelva going first, then his daughter Laurel, then his wife Fay, they walked into the windowless room where the doctor would make his examination."

In the next paragraphs, though the narrative stays in the scene—concentrating on how everybody looks, what they say and do—we are unobtrusively given some facts: Laurel is "in her middle forties." "New Orleans was out-of-town for all of them." That's such an important sentence; otherwise, of course, we'd assume at least one of them lived there. As it is, we wait patiently until we're told why they've come to a place where none of them lives. We don't know, but we're not confused. We don't make wrong assumptions—except about the dead mother, whose story is told in hints so oblique that some readers miss them; she is still being silenced.

In Alice Munro's story "Cortes Island," a bitter woman keeps the narrator from living honestly, speaking out, and, at least temporarily, becoming a writer. The woman and her young husband live in a basement apartment in Vancouver. The time is the 1950s, and upstairs live Mr. and Mrs. Gorrie. The narrator pretends to look for a job, but she doesn't want to find one. She is writing: she tells people she's writing letters, but she's writing stories, which are failures. She writes the same thing over and over again, tears the pages out of a notebook, and stuffs them in the trash. When no pages are left, she buys a new notebook. Eventually it turns out that Mrs. Gorrie has come into the apartment while the narrator was out, and read the trash: when she's angry with the narrator for other reasons, she mocks these attempted stories and says the narrator is crazy.

Mrs. Gorrie advocates femininity: dressing up, wearing makeup, obsessive baking and cleaning. Her baked goods are inedible, but she often forces the narrator, who would rather be reading or writing, to come upstairs and eat them. As the story proceeds, there are hints that the narrator's husband, Chess, also values housekeeping and material objects. They have married because sex was impossible otherwise, but now their goal becomes material advancement. When the narrator finally gets a job, in the library, they move to a bigger apartment; with two salaries they can afford it. The narrator is willing. She is glad to have escaped from the failure-ridden inner life she has been leading, haunted by the dreadful Mrs. Gorrie and her husband, an invalid who had a stroke and cannot speak—as the narrator is symbolically prevented from speaking. Only faintly does the story hint that she's making the wrong choice, that she is wrong to give up writing stories to become "the girl in the library": someone with a clear function that everyone understands. She is shelving and checking out books instead of reading and writing them.

Having moved away, the narrator forgets about Mrs. Gorrie, but for years she has erotic dreams about Mr. Gorrie. We're allowed to understand that eventually she leaves the marriage, and since what we're reading is a story, we conclude that she returned to writing stories—and, perhaps, became some version of Alice Munro. For the present, though, her dreams about her silenced neighbor are the only proof of remaining life. The character, censored by others, has censored herself, and the writing has ceased.

Munro is a strikingly outspoken writer. In her stories we usually know just what's what; they are longer than most people's. But she uses indirection here just enough to establish an intimate tone, as if the reader is a friend of hers. At the beginning the narrator refers to "Chess" and the office he works in. She doesn't say, "Chess was my husband," or "Chess worked in an office," and those additions might make the story a little more formal.

The most interesting ellipsis is a hidden story. For a time, the narrator takes care of the mute Mr. Gorrie, upstairs, while his wife is out. Through gestures, he directs her to look through some scrapbooks, and the newspaper articles he wants her to see are about the death of a man in a house in the woods on Cortes

Island, a wild area north of Vancouver. The man died in a fire; the fire might have been set. The man's wife was away, on a boat with a friend. In one article the friend is unidentified, but in a second one he's named: it's Mr. Gorrie. So the dead man's wife was the present Mrs. Gorrie of the inedible cookies, and indeed she has told the narrator that she once lived in the wilds. That's all—but we know as if it were stated that Mr. and Mrs. Gorrie were adulterous lovers who killed Mrs. Gorrie's first husband or drove him to kill himself—and got away with it, except that now Mrs. Gorrie leads not a glamorous life of love and dramatic deeds but an unhappy domestic one.

This reticence is thrilling, and if it arises out of the constraint that people like the narrator of "Cortes Island" feel, so much the better: maybe some things *are* unspeakable. The hidden story is powerful, and partly I think it's because we as readers, who have not had it told to us, feel as if we with our dirty minds have invented it—we become complicit.

Telling the Story

Elliptical writing, nonrealistic writing, indirect writing, writing that somehow confuses the reader on purpose—all can be exciting and dramatic, but that doesn't mean a direct, clear, realistic story is any less powerful. I've come to think that writing directly is usually *more* powerful than writing indirectly, and when it has problems, they are easier to see. But if you prefer something else, I don't have a problem as your reader. It's when you make the choice to do something else because you're afraid, that you should suspect your motives—and I will become impatient with your story. Writing is full of legitimate difficulty, and as we write a story we may have anxieties we can't dispel, but we needn't allow them to determine our aesthetic choices.

As we write, I believe we should recognize that we probably are being censored, if not by a government, then perhaps by publishers who impose standards that may not always be conducive to the making of art, often—especially if we are women—by people who are close to us, and most of all by ourselves. Governments would not be able to persecute writers if people did not censor one another and themselves in private life, just as officially sanctioned racism, sexism, or homophobia depends on the existence of private fear and hatred. The lesson for us is clear. If, at some time in our lives, telling a story plainly puts us in danger of prison or death, we should make sure our memberships in PEN, the Authors Guild, and the ACLU are current (we should anyway), fight for our right to speak—and, meanwhile, consider not telling the story, or telling it so obliquely or strangely that nobody can prove what we meant. If pretending not to tell the story by telling it indirectly or unrealistically, or hinting at it or leaving parts out will make it clearer and stronger, then we should follow those impulses. But let's not tell stories elliptically or indirectly or unrealistically for the wrong reasons. Let's try to ignore censoring voices around us and inside us, and take on the authority of the person we call the author, the person in charge. Let's tell the story.

PART V

Living to Tell the Tale

CHAPTER 9

Revising Our Thought Bubbles

The Fantasy

Not long ago I had surgery for a hernia, and I persuaded the doctors not to give me a drug that would make me forget the whole thing later, so I remember just what happened. As the surgeon and nurses were working on my belly, the anesthesiologist leaned over and said, in a kind, heavily accented voice, "I hear you are writer."

"Yes." This topic was not, at that moment, what I most wanted to talk about.

"Wow," a nurse behind me said. "What do you write?"

"Oh, God," I thought. I said, "I'm a novelist."

Flurry of interest around the table. Then a different nurse said, "Anything we've heard of?"

There's a pervasive idea that if you're actually a writer, almost anyone will have heard of you and your books—an idea that becomes laughable to anyone who's looked left and right in a Barnes & Noble or browsed through online booksellers' wares. Nobody has heard of more than a tiny fraction of all those writers or their books. Still, many people who aren't writers persist in thinking of authors as rare, distinguished creatures—maybe a little repellent because we are able to bring to life what isn't there and are unafraid of strong feeling: you never know what a writer will say next. Repellent, possibly, but always happy, like some people's unendurably successful children. When we then write something—we writers—we surely cannot help, at some level, thinking that people will line up to read what we've written, give us money and praise and honor. Operating room nurses will recognize the titles of our books.

Meanwhile, it becomes harder to publish, and for a published book to find readers. Publishers, for reasons we can understand even if we don't like them, spend most of their budget for promotion on books they believe are potential best sellers, and one result is that many readers think those—the books they've heard of through ads and interviews and big promotions—are the only books that exist. So surely, if you've really written a book, they'll know about it.

Yet crowds of us who want to be writers converge on MFA programs, writers' conferences, undergraduate writing departments, and informal groups—or just sit alone and write. And above nearly all our heads (not quite all) floats the same thought bubble, one of those little balloons linked by a string of circles to the back of a cartoon head. We're all picturing a best-selling, well-received book, published by a mainstream press, and providing enough money for the author to live on while staying home and writing more books.

Which means that nearly all of us are disappointed nearly all the time. Most writers earn little or no money. A few get advances for first books that are large enough, after taxes, for them to live in modest comfort while they write second books, but even they often don't get the same kind of money again. They'll never again be as young and new, and maybe that first book didn't sell quite as well as the editor had hoped. Publishers and agents must aim high—any businessperson has to. A publisher or agent accepts many books, hoping that one will do extremely well. A writing program is thrilled when a few of its alumni get rich and famous. But what is to sustain the other writers, emotionally and financially? Even when it's published, most writing brings in, if anything, the occasional windfall, delightful when it comes, making possible treats and long-postponed projects ranging from dinner out to a weekend trip to a new roof to—rarely—a few months of unpaid leave, but not large or predictable enough for us to quit our day jobs. Writers manage by working at something else (which is sometimes teaching writing at a university), inheriting a fortune, or relying on a partner with a steady job.

For new writers who have indulged in the usual fantasy, it's a shock to discover that there are *not* just a few writers, each being made much of all day long forever, but, rather, far too many to count. The shock makes some people competitive and unpleasant, and they become embittered loners sneering at successful authors, detecting unfairness in every rejection. Other new writers, feeling less entitled, reason, "What are the odds that stupid old me, who forgot to buy laundry detergent so she's wearing the same underwear for the third day in a row, will be one of the successful few?" and give up trying. This last chapter is about finding a way of thinking somewhere between the delusion that we will all achieve spectacular success and the delusion that we are all doomed to sickening failure.

Revising our thought bubbles—finding more accurate and satisfying ways to describe to ourselves who we are, what we're attempting, and what we want—is a task we face together, at least as important as our other big jobs as a community of writers, like promoting the reading of good books and fighting to preserve independent bookstores. Nobody's going to help us work on the fantasy. Publishers and agents benefit from the myth that writers are glamorous, and readers like to think of the authors they admire as people of substance, if not spectacular wealth. When a newspaper story reports the presence of writers at an event, the ones it names are, naturally, those you've heard of—perpetuating the fantasy that famous writers are the only writers. It can be hard to convince people that we aren't all successful all the time. Even my students, a generally canny bunch, express astonishment if they learn that my stories are repeatedly rejected and my novels have mostly sold badly.

The result of all this stubborn fantasizing is that writers make demands on themselves that they cannot meet—sometimes not realizing that virtually nobody meets them—and then, all too often, suffer shame and depression. People who have published well in magazines beat themselves up for not having a book, and people who've published books consider themselves failures because they haven't published enough books, or the right sort of books, or extremely successful books. Someone who has a big success with a first novel may have trouble with the second and never try a third. On the other hand, people who publish well but earn a living at something other than writing may not feel sure they're really writers. And a few established writers speak of anyone who starts writing in middle age, or earns a living at something other than writing, or doesn't publish often—or is working seriously at writing but hasn't published yet—as a "hobbyist." There *are* hobbyists—they write just for themselves or for their friends and families, for the pleasure of self-expression. There's nothing wrong with writing as a hobby, but that's not what we're discussing here. Writers revise their work, struggling with it, trying to make it something strangers will want to read. People who work hard at writing and eventually publish, whether obscurely or famously, in journals or in book form—as long as some serious person has made the decision to bring out their work—are surely writers, as people who play music in public are musicians, whether they earn a good living at it or perform only occasionally while working at something else. The way to recognize hobbyists is that they're light-hearted. People in danger of suicide because their writing careers are going badly are not hobbyists.

What Shall We Do?

It would be crazy to give up the fantasy entirely: after all, some people *do* get money and prizes—why not you or I? *Somebody* reading this book will become spectacularly successful as a writer, and maybe even hold on to success. There's nothing wrong with hoping and daydreaming. It's just that it makes no sense to require that outcome for ourselves, and feel angry, ashamed, or depressed when we don't achieve it.

Nor, I think, should we aim for philosophical detachment. Writers have said to me more than once, "I have wonderful, healthy children—I shouldn't also need to publish my novel." We shouldn't *give up* the desire to be successful as if it were shameful and greedy; we shouldn't regard publication as something to sacrifice for our spiritual development. We write to be read: we should want to be read and try to be read.

All this bad thinking—whether it's the assumption that every writer is famous, that you're rejected because publishers hate you, that you're rejected because you're worthless, that it's a character flaw to want to publish or publish well or be paid decently—indicates a misconception about writing that many new writers (and nonwriters) hold, the misconception that writing is a phenomenon out of a fairy tale, more romantic than everyday life: the fancy wedding rather than the marriage. Telling people I'm a writer often evokes the kind of "Ooh!" that seems more appropriate for a child's achievement (except that it also feels hostile). New writers don't want to hear that my day was a slog, that publication involves as many disappointments as triumphs, that my job isn't totally different from theirs. Being a writer is a profession, not the last scene of a romantic comedy.

It's understandable that people who earn their living doing something they don't like much, who write only on weekends or during vacations, should start to think about writing the way they may think about falling in love: as something that comes mysteriously if at all but, if it does come, can change a life. And it's certainly true that writing is a joy when it goes well, and publishing can feel great. But it's not a good idea to think of writing something you hope to publish as offering your truest self to the world, hoping for love and affirmation. Editors, publishers, and agents are in business. What they do when they consider our writing is work, even if it's unpaid work (often the case at literary magazines and small presses) or work done idealistically by agents or editors who care enough about good writing that they risk losing money by representing or publishing what may not sell well. What a writer does is also work—a job, whether full- or part-time—and offering it for publication is not the same as what happens when a child presents a painting to a parent in exchange for kisses and praise; it's dangerous to think it is.

Submitting writing for publication isn't completely unlike selling a house. Selling a house, to be sure, is difficult. Like writing, it has personal elements, and it can be tempting to think of a rejection of your house not as a rejection of square footage or layout but as a rejection of your life and choices. But if we have any sense, when we sell a house, we try to minimize the ways in which the process will feel like a personal attack or a personal compliment. A piece of writing too may begin with what's personal, but by the time we offer it for publication, we had better think of it as a work product. We should have revised it until we've become detached enough that if it's turned down, we'll decide that maybe the beginning is confusing after all. Or maybe the end needs work. In any case, we will not collapse in a heap and think our lives are over because nobody cares about the subject we've written about—or, thus, about us.

If you own a store, you don't take to your bed each time a potential customer looks something over and walks out empty-handed. If you did, you'd soon go bankrupt from sheer anxiety. Like someone going into business, we must develop goals that make sense for us, and feel happy and unhappy as we meet or fail to meet them. We need the mind-set of the working person, who may think, "To do this job right, I need a computer with more memory" or "an assistant" or "a bigger lab," but who does *not* then think, "Oh, but I should be grateful for what I have—my nice spouse and children." People who have written books, worked hard to make them good, and revised them again and again *should* want to publish them. Maybe they won't get what they want, or not without additional struggle, but maybe the person at work won't get the bigger lab or the assistant either. It's a disappointment but not a personal judgment.

At work we seem to have little trouble keeping in mind two sorts of hopes, two sorts of fantasies: the one we can strive for and achieve, and the one that's unlikely but fun to think about. Writers too need plausible and implausible goals, and should learn to judge themselves and possibly change their behavior based on the plausible ones.

And the less our goals involve money, the likelier it is that we can achieve them—which is unfair and awful. Don't get me wrong: if what you write is worth reading, you *should* be paid, and you should do all you can to get the money that society owes you, or would owe you in a fairer system. Don't give away your time and talent to people who can afford to pay you for it. Participate in the efforts of organizations that work to get writers the money they should have.

But don't make money the goal by which you judge yourself. Novelists and nonfiction authors get advances ranging from almost nothing (at some small presses) to many millions, based on somebody's assessment of potential sales: even if your book is published by a mainstream house, you may earn less than 1 percent of what some other author makes, quite apart from merit. If you sell a story to the *New Yorker*, you'll get thousands of dollars, and if you sell it to a typical literary magazine, you'll get a few hundred, or nothing. Somehow we need to learn to participate in the publishing business without surrendering to it emotionally—without coming to believe that money and excellence are invariably connected, or that something is wrong with us if we can't get a lot of money from writing. The trick is to be angry without being destroyed by anger, to be sad without thinking that maybe the tiny sum you just got for the story you worked on for years is all you deserve.

There is no solution, no guaranteed justice—but we can chip away at the discontent. Your writing is not your child; it's work, but unfortunately a kind of work that is often unpaid, badly paid, or weirdly paid: writers who make lots of money are often as baffled as the rest of us. If you want to write and publish, there are truths you need to get used to: you'll probably always need to make a living at something else (though possibly at a combination of writing and teaching writing); and the money, though there may be some, will never make sense. That's just the way it is.

OK. If you can stop getting involved emotionally in a system that doesn't make much sense, if you can stop taking personally what doesn't actually have to do with you—then you can begin to choose realistic goals and work toward them. Writing itself will be as pleasurable as ever. But publication will stop being the end of a fairy tale, for you or others. It will lose glamour. People say to me, "Oh, you have a book coming out—you must be so thrilled!" and if you follow the advice I'm offering here, you'll lose part of the expectation of that thrill for yourself, and part of the vicarious thrill for others. Having a book come out is exciting, of course—it's *great* to see your name on a book jacket, to see your book in a store—but it's also risky and scary and tiring. Publishing a book is not becoming a child again and winning a medal with a little ribbon on it. It's part of a satisfying but difficult job, going from being alone with your work to having others work on it—others you may not always like or agree with, and who, like any business contacts, may be brilliant and helpful, or irritating and insensitive. The book may sell well—or not. I imagine that publishing a book is something like being made the president of a college. Nobody ever says to the new president, "Oh, you must be so thrilled!" though of course it's a huge honor. "Congratulations," we say, "and good luck, ha ha! You'll need it!"

If you think of writing and publishing as work, you'll gush less and suffer less. You may be angry and disappointed—but it won't get to you as keenly. The bad parts are like your boss disapproving of you, not like your parents abandoning you. Giving up the fantasy of bliss does not mean becoming satisfied with what you have. It means understanding realistically why you don't have what you don't have, whether you might get it if you did some things differently, and whether that would be worth it to you.

Figure Out What You Actually Want

Whatever you may think of capitalism as an economic system, you probably already judge some capitalistic values skeptically. You don't take the business community's word for how many toys a child needs or which car will improve your sex life. Capitalism also offers a definition of a successful author, but we don't have to believe that either.

I happen to be the absolutely last person to hear about whatever is big in popular culture. At a party—if I'm actually invited to one and actually go—instinctively I choose the least glamorous, least powerful person in the room to talk to. Though I've managed to have a writing career, I don't seem to make choices that lead to stardom. I'm just not made that way, and maybe you're not either, and maybe we can stand that. If what you like best, besides the blessed, solitary task itself, is the community of minds that writing offers, the pleasures of cooperation rather than competition, then don't make yourself miserable wishing for a kind of success that you wouldn't enjoy if you had it. Daydream about good things you'd like—readings for small but receptive audiences, editing that helps you understand what you wanted to say, e-mails from friends and strangers who have understood your story.

Think, too, about what kind of writing schedule would be ideal for you: again, decide what to want. Since I became serious about writing, I've wanted most weekdays free to write, and much of the time, making some sacrifices, I've been able to get that. I thought I wanted it, and I did—I like my empty days with the dog; I write. Maybe you're like me, and if so, maybe you can manage to get a life similar to mine—and I am sorry if you want a life like this but can't get it.

But maybe you don't want it. Having the day free for writing is part of the myth about what we want, but is it actually what *you* want? A painter in my neighborhood was married to a teacher. They decided to live cheaply so he could paint full time, and for a time he stayed home. But when he was offered a teaching job, he grabbed it. He said, "I'm sure the mailman wonders what I do." If you stay home and work on any kind of art, you probably make little money, and you look like someone loafing. Do you care about that? Many people need outside contacts, professional connections, a place to go. Even I can't do without teaching, and for twenty-four years I worked at a soup kitchen once a week. When I arrived, people looked up and nodded: I belonged there. I seemed to need that nod. Writers have to feel that they matter, and while staying home in stained jeans (or pajamas) can be liberating, it can also be a way of declaring that you don't matter—which can't be good for the work.

Psychologically, you may need to go to a job and perform satisfactorily at it, at least some of the time, even if you don't need the money. Deriving self-esteem solely from success in writing is—at least for me and many others I know—too hard. The highs and lows are intense: you're being published or you're being rejected; the reviewer loves your book or hates it; you won the prize or you didn't win the prize—a prize you never heard of until last month, but now that you've heard of it and haven't won it, you feel like a failure. And so on. I don't know about you, but I need the tamer joys and sorrows of less competitive work—teaching, in my case— to balance those thrills and downfalls.

I know people who have full-time jobs and dream of being full-time writers but who would hate it. They already do badly with unstructured time. When they don't go to work, they give up exercising and eat badly, waste time, and write little. Sometimes it's easier to make writing happen when time is limited.

If you're someone who would do well having nothing to succeed at but writing and having your time free for it, OK, never mind, go back to the daydream. But if you aren't, stop telling everyone how sad it is that you can't quit your job and "just write." If a limited amount of additional free time would benefit you, maybe you can get that. I know a weaver who took a day job in an office years ago that she still has. From the first, she negotiated the right to take occasional unpaid weeks off to work at her loom. She has probably advanced less at that job than if she'd made it her priority, but she doesn't regret that, and she's become an extremely good and successful weaver. Maybe you too can change your hours, use vacation time differently, or finagle something else beneficial. That is a goal worth focusing on. Find the best available solution for you, and try to get it.

What Shall We Not Do?

As we decide on goals for publication and how to achieve them, first, let's make up our minds not to become Cinderella's wicked stepsisters (and brothers). That is, let's not be mean; let's not look down at others who don't have what we have; let's not brag; let's not regard other writers as competitors for the same scrap of success. We should look for ways to be generous rather than greedy, and help along young people and those starting out.

But also—and this is the greater risk for people reading this book, I suspect—let's not be Cinderella. Part of what makes that fairy tale powerful is the prince, who swoops up Cinderella into a life of luxury and love—in our terms, into a glorious literary career. (I suppose that in our "Cinderella" the prince is an editor and the fairy godmother is an agent.) But the story's potency also depends on Cinderella herself—the ragged, dirty girl humbly sweeping up ashes until she's rescued. She is never the wicked stepsisters' cleaning woman, a person with a business, a calendar, and a modicum of dignity, though she may dislike having to scrub fireplaces. The story requires Cinderella to be wretched—though how this sooty menial will manage the household staff and diplomatic dinners at the castle I do not know. And indeed, if you insist on playing Cinderella until an agent and editor transform you, you won't be much of a manager either. All you'll have in your repertory is humility when your publisher suggests a jacket design that you loathe.

I've seen too many new writers (and writers who aren't so new) play Cinderella—that is, put themselves into a humbler situation than makes sense. We can't make publication easy or entirely fair, but let's not make it harder than it is. When a workshop or a competent teacher tells you your manuscript needs work, work on it: it has strengths and weaknesses, and whoever has critiqued it is not trying to find a nice way to say it's worthless. If someone with experience suggests that your work is publishable, *send it out*—don't think, "She's just being kind."

When a magazine rejects a piece of writing but says, "Please try us again," *try them again*. If you get another rejection, feel sad, sure—but don't spiral down into despair and self-doubt.

Don't revise work past the point at which you're improving it. Revise it many times—but then show it to friends, and after a few more revisions, if it seems done, send it out. I've written thirty drafts of some stories. Poets sometimes write one hundred drafts. But don't revise just because you can't imagine that you could ever finish anything.

I know accomplished writers in their forties and fifties who have been regarding themselves as apprentices for decades. Don't keep going to writing school. Writing school is good—it may be just the right thing for you—but you don't need school after school, class after class, teacher after teacher forever. If you're actually writing publishable work—you know what that means, but it's our next topic in any case—then get out there and try. Yes, submitting manuscripts is difficult, but it's not going to get easier if you revise that story for another ten years.

Is Your Work Good Enough to Publish?

Obviously I can't answer that question, but I can make some suggestions about the process of deciding. Like everything else about writing, deciding whether and where to try to publish involves being emotionally free at times and using common sense at other times—flying a kite, hanging on to a string—and as with everything else, the trick is not to be carried away by feeling, especially negative feeling, when you need common sense, and not to let an understandable desire for order and process keep you from facing up to larger issues.

If you're writing seriously for readers, the time will come when you'll feel ready to find them. I read and wrote poems all my life, but didn't send any out. When my oldest child was a year old, I hired a sitter to come four hours a week and look after him, so I could write poems in the basement. Suddenly writing felt non-negotiable. I wrote a few poems in which I unleashed feeling on the page in a way I never had before, and after a couple of months of that, I decided to send poems out. I don't remember why, but I think I must have had something like the hitherto recreational gambler's realization that she's just gambled the mortgage payment. Writing, I've been told, is a "benign addiction." There was certainly something like the feeling that I was in it for real, risking what mattered, already risking more emotionally by writing the poems than I would by submitting them—so I ought to try to get whatever rewards were available. Maybe I wanted money to pay the babysitter. I did get one of those new poems published, and was paid thirty-five dollars, the first money I earned from writing. Three years and a million rejections later, I sold another one for seventy-five dollars. After that it got a bit easier.

So the first question to ask yourself, if you're thinking about publication, is Am I gambling the mortgage? In other words, are these stories messy and embarrassing, emotionally costly? Am I discovering what's unexpected and even frightening in myself as I write?

The next question: Am I open enough, after I gamble the mortgage, to face what's wrong with the stories and fix it? Am I revising to make my work something readers will want to read (rather than writing just to unburden myself)? Revision is a big subject, and deserves a little more attention.

Revising Without Despair

The difference between writers and people who say they are writers but aren't may be that writers assume they'll revise. For me and most of the writers I know, first drafts are exciting, suspenseful— will anything come at all?—and painful. There are moments of doubt, though as we grow older and more experienced, those moments are more pleasant than they used to be, more like moments of suspense in a movie: though they can be sickeningly real, for the most part they just make life a bit more exciting. When the first draft is done, something is lost—but it's such a relief. Working on something is easier than working on nothing. I hope you too like to revise.

But how? To learn how to revise effectively, you must, to the extent possible, learn to see your work as a stranger would, and *that* requires, first, the confidence (which you may have to fake) that some things in this work are already right—that it has strengths as well as weaknesses. If you've read this far—if you're that serious—of course it does. Second, it requires a certain casualness. A stranger reading your work wouldn't feel that your worth and dignity hung on the merit of every word on these pages, so you mustn't either. Maybe the pages are no good. OK, you'll fix them.

To read your work objectively as that stranger, it's helpful to surprise your piece of writing into thinking you're someone else. To do that, put it aside for anywhere from a day to three years, the longer the better (up to a point). Then take it to a part of your house where you never write, or go elsewhere, and wear something unusual so it won't recognize you—a cap, perhaps, or a jaunty scarf, especially if you are *not* jaunty. Then read it slowly, looking for clichés to get rid of, awkward or illogical sentences, places where a reader who didn't know what you know about the layout of the town or the composition of the family might be confused, places where it gets slow or sentimental or melodramatic—and especially for what makes it a story, what makes it matter and move along, what makes it complete.

Read your work as if you were new to it. Notice when you're restless, bored, or resistant. Have you (as the author) shifted to a different time or viewpoint though the reader (you, at present) wants a little more time where you were? Is this shift too abrupt, or, perhaps, do you *want* abrupt here? As the reader, you should be informed, pleasantly mystified, curious, horrified, amused—are you? Sometimes the greatest suspense comes when readers know what's going to happen but must wait for it; sometimes knowing what's going to happen spoils the fun. If you've observed what keeps you reading in the books you love, you can look for some of that in your own work.

As you read your work, note divisions into paragraphs and sections. Fix your paragraphs so they end when you don't mind if the reader glances up from the book. End a chapter when you don't mind if your reader goes to the bathroom, has a snack, or puts the book down until the next day.

If, as you read, you suddenly realize the whole thing is garbage, I promise you, it isn't. This happens, and it's never real; you wouldn't have devoted all that time to it if it were garbage. Put the piece aside for a few hours, calm down, and try again. Maybe then you can see clearly what it needs and what is all right as it is. What misleading sentence dooms the next ten pages—but can be taken out? Or maybe the ten pages themselves have to go. If you still can't tell, get one of your writer friends—someone who knows what an early draft is!—to read it, armed with a series of questions.

Let's assume you've been able to distinguish between what's working and what isn't, with a friend's help or on your own, and you have some goals as you sit down to revise, more than just fixing the spelling. It's helpful to retype your work at least once, on a blank screen—as we gray-haired writers did in the days of typewriters. Your fingers may balk at a bad sentence your mind would let pass. When you retype a story on a blank screen, new thoughts will slide through your typing fingers onto the page and appear there unexpectedly. Retyping preserves spontaneity even in this rational process; it keeps the kite flying, because it allows your unconscious mind some play. When you come to a passage you were planning to paste into the new file without changes, begin copying it instead—and suddenly you may see that you ought to change it after all. If you've made the daughter slightly more or slightly less unreasonable in the early scene when she borrows the car and has an accident, the father's memory of that day, one hundred pages later, may call up a different image, require a different adjective, have a different tone. If you've decided that the daughter was injured—not just shaken up—everyone from the police officer to the driver of the other car will speak of the incident in a somewhat different way. It's relaxing to retype—less stressful than trying to be brilliant at every moment.

It's also helpful to read your work on paper, not just on the screen, and to read it aloud.

If you decide to move the parts of your story around—and you should consider reorganizing it instead of just assuming that the structure you landed on first is the correct one—it's far easier to keep from getting mixed up if you cut and paste physically rather than electronically. In general, computers make things easier, but settling down with scissors and tape or glue, spreading the parts of your story out on the kitchen table, is fun, and often less confusing than performing that task electronically. Routine tasks are calming, and calm is a state of mind in which ideas come. Don't invariably welcome technology's capacity to remove repetitive action from the writing process. As you know if you regularly get ideas while gardening or cleaning the house, physical work, if it's not too difficult, liberates thought.

I write several drafts before I show anyone what I'm doing, which doesn't mean *you* should, but think about it. I was recently talking with a student whose work was always good, but some-times a little studied, a little unspontaneous. The most recent story I'd seen, though, was much better—emotionally free and open, full of surprises. When I said so, she told me that she usually discussed her work with her husband, a scientist, before she wrote, and he was helpful and friendly about it. This time, though, she'd been too rushed—she'd told no one about the new story. It seemed that however wonderful that husband is, he was constraining her a little, maybe making her a little self-conscious, too polite. Maybe, not being a writer, he was encouraging her to make the story too tidy at the outset; he didn't see the need for all those messy drafts. She'll be better off when she saves him for later.

Finding Readers

Another question to ask yourself as you consider trying to publish: Have you found people willing to read your work and think about it—in a classroom setting or informally—who can tell you what's wrong and what you might do about it? You may need to make changes in your life to find good readers, and sometimes it takes many tries. I never went to writing school, but I had friends who were writers. Still, I had to try many friends and several groups before I found the people who could help me— a friend from college, friends I met because our children were the same age, poets I met through the writing of poetry, a musician with a good eye for words. If you go to writing school (it's an excellent way to join a community of writers large enough that you'll surely find friends and writing partners), avoid programs that promise that you'll publish; no one can promise that. Look for those that emphasize reading, including the literature of the past; learn from writers who have done it best over the centuries. Choose between residency and low-residency programs. Studying in a residency program may require you to relocate, but may offer more opportunities to teach while you're a student. A low-residency program is ideal if you have a job, children, or other reasons to stay where you now live, since you'll need to be at the college for only a few weeks a year, corresponding with a teacher in between, and residencies are generally scheduled for times when it's not hard to take a vacation. You'll probably find committed teachers and new friends wherever you go.

Once you're in school, don't take in criticism as Cinderella, as someone prepared to be humiliated. Welcome it and figure out in advance what you want to learn from it. It's thrilling when someone can help you with what you've written.

If you don't go to writing school, it will be worthwhile to take some trouble to solve the problem of finding readers. Study your relatives and friends; maybe join an informal writing group. Finding other writers is good, because it's less nerve-racking to exchange work than to ask the nonwriters in your life to read your writing when you can't reciprocate. But not all groups are helpful. When I was starting out, I joined a local group in which, it turned out, hardly anyone wrote anything. I began to feel self-conscious about always bringing new work, as if I were showing off. I dropped out.

After that, for thirteen years I was in a writing workshop with two poets, Jane Kenyon and Joyce Peseroff; it ended when Jane died of leukemia at age forty-seven. We met three or four times a year at one of our widely separated houses—Jane lived in New Hampshire, Joyce in Massachusetts, and I in Connecticut—spent the night, and worked on what we'd brought—their poems; my poems and later my fiction—for a day and a half. We talked about everything: freedom of imagination, tiny little problems in wording and structure, lack of confidence. The workshop made me dare to be a writer.

It's possible to show your writing, cautiously, to people who aren't writers and to learn from them. The important word is "cautiously." I hear too many stories about shame and despair after a new writer shows what he or she has written to a family member or friend—and somehow this seems to be one area in which men are more vulnerable or less careful than women: all the sad stories I've heard about giving up on a novel because of what a relative said have been told to me by men. I think men should be especially careful about showing early drafts of their novels to their fathers, though, like all rules, this one should be broken in the right circumstances.

I don't think it's a problem—far from it—if your mother, father, sibling, cousin, spouse, friend, or lover likes your work too much. Too much praise is wonderful, like too much money. For years my husband insisted, when asked—usually in the middle of the night—that my work would someday be published, and my loyal cousin Arnie was stubbornly certain of my greatness. Don't rush to send your novel to an agent as soon as your cousin tells you it's brilliant—but hug and kiss your cousin, because he may have noticed something.

Cherish the readers who offer more praise than you deserve, but find others as well—which may be more difficult. A critique should make you want to get back to work. If it makes you want to quit, don't turn to that reader again, no matter who he or she is and how hard it will be in the future to deal with questions like "When can I see your new story?" (If you can't bear to say "Never!" or "I've decided to work a little differently," say, "Hmmm . . . I don't really know." Then glance at your phone as if checking your calendar and shake your head slowly, in bafflement at your own unpredictable habits.)

Protect yourself in advance, when showing your work, by giving your reader a list of instructions, maybe in writing—instructions like "Please note in the margin if you're confused. Please note if you're reading something you already know. Please note when you figure out the ending. Please note if you laugh." Specific criticism won't hurt as much as general rejection. Don't ask, "Do you hate it? You hate it, don't you?" If your reader seems to have something more to say after giving you specific responses to pages and paragraphs, and isn't burbling with joy, cautiously try to find out why—but again, keep it specific and objective. "Something's bothering you about the story. Did anything seem implausible? Did you dislike the characters?" It may not be a problem if your reader dislikes the characters, but you'd probably just as soon know. And often when readers need to unburden themselves, at least about my work, that's what they finally want to confess: they don't like everything my characters *do*. Well, neither do I—that's why I'm writing about them. The criticism tells me more about the reader than about my work; some readers want a degree of idealization of life that doesn't interest me. On the other hand, sometimes I've made my characters *too* flawed. I haven't yet put in enough good moments to make them lovable as well.

Friends who critique your work may hesitate and apologize, then tell you something that isn't terrible news at all, just an indication that you need to rewrite, which is what you expected: the plot events don't feel plausible yet, the writing needs to be toned down, the ending is too easy to see coming, the theme is too blatant or so subtle the reader doesn't know what it is. All fixable. Sometimes readers get tremendously upset and then confess that your draft has a tiny mistake—you've made your character take the Fifth Avenue bus in New York uptown, but Fifth Avenue is *one way*, running *downtown*! Manage your readers, especially if they aren't writers but even if they are. Guide the discussion—stay in charge.

The best critics are often the other writers with whom you exchange work, both because they are likelier to know how you might fix what's wrong and because they know that *they* will be showing *you* a manuscript soon enough. Whatever has gone wrong in their lives, they are not as likely to take it out on your poor story if their own will get the same treatment. Other writers do have one disadvantage as critics: they are sometimes too quick to propose fixing a problem the way *they* would fix it. But you can recognize that, and find your own solution. You need to learn from your readers what gives them trouble, but you may have to think hard about what they *say* to understand what the actual difficulty is, or that there isn't any.

Learn how to hear criticism so as to use it or discard it. The reader who says, "Take out the brother," probably means that you've mentioned a brother, but not given him enough of a role in the story to justify his presence. When another reader says, "I want more of the brother," that's the same message: if you're going to keep this brother, give him more to do. Decide what to do not by paying attention to everything you're told, but by following the bit of advice that comes alive when you hear it, and from what you yourself observe, judge, and want. Solve problems when you're wide awake and your sense of humor is engaged.

I revise again and again, but often I still haven't revised enough. It's hard to know when your own work is finished. My stories are regularly rejected after my friends and I have decided they are done. Eventually I may figure out what's wrong, or some helpful editor who rejects the story may give me a hint. And I revise yet again. And again. Novels—such complicated creatures—need even more revising. Yet I meet writers who are dismayed that their stories and novels need to be revised. They are hurt and disappointed—or they are bravely humble and ashamed, as if they are the only people who can't do something everyone else does easily. Writing isn't something you can get straight once and for all, like tying your shoelaces. Dancers and musicians have teachers well into their professional careers. They expect and welcome teaching. Writers, too, can never entirely learn to see the flaws in their own work. That's why editors exist; many agents are also good early readers. There's no such thing as a writer who doesn't need editing, and if you don't have—or don't yet have—the benefit of professional editors and agents, you'll need to find help somewhere else. Even when you do have professionals, there's still no substitute for showing your work to your friends. You'll always need them.

It's not bad news that your work needs revision; it's the nature of writing. Just because you've already revised your piece many times doesn't prove it's done. On the other hand, the fact that it's not yet right after many tries also doesn't mean it's hopeless. We practice a difficult art. Someone who has been unable to publish three or four novels and is on the third draft of her current novel may *still* have to start over, and even that doesn't mean she's hopeless or the book is hopeless. On the contrary, she may finally be on the verge of learning to write a novel—yet that often seems to be the moment when she decides to give up.

"I may throw it out the window," a woman in a workshop said recently about a novel that we all thought had a great idea at its center, but not much else so far. We'd seen other work of hers, and she was an excellent writer. She'd been writing this novel—and novels before it—for quite a while. Not that I blame her for possibly giving up, if she can. Reworking a long novel yet again may just not be worth it. There's nothing wrong with that choice, though it will be painful—it's like deciding not to buy a dilapidated house with great potential, or not to spend time with a demanding if at times rewarding friend. At times the choice to give up may be sensible, and a relief in the long run.

However—I'll say it again—the fact that a story or novel has been revised many times but still needs a few more drafts doesn't prove a thing, and *certainly* not that it will never be any good.

Learn to Write by Reading

The next question, when you're deciding whether your work may be publishable, is whether you're reading enough, have read enough, whether you've worked into your bones whatever the truths are about the sort of writing you're doing. If you're writing stories, have you read the likes of Chekhov, Turgenev, Henry James, James Joyce, Katherine Mansfield—or at least a few of them—up through the interesting books of stories being published as we speak? And likewise for the novel, for poems, for personal essays and memoir. Of course, you can't read everything—but are you reading with curiosity, with a willingness to see what some authors can do that you can't (or can't yet), and with intellectual energy?

We figure out in the first place what we want to write because of what we've read. Few of us can invent a new form. We know about novels because we've read novels, about poems because we've read poems. But sometimes people who are writing short stories read only novels—how will they learn what the possibilities are? I don't mean that reading offers instructions we take in consciously. Having read piles of short stories, you may reread one of yours and think, "No, it doesn't quite get there. It doesn't behave like a story."

Resist the efforts of the publishing industry to make you read only the books that are already popular. You may be writing a good book that won't appeal to multitudes, and you should look for other books that will appeal to only a few—including, as it happens, you.

We have to read all the time, and not just the books that we already know will be our favorites. If we keep reading widely and deeply, we'll start to prefer what we know is good. Tired plot devices will tire us and clichés will bore us, while complicated reasoning or language of past centuries will be easier to follow. It's important to read diversely—to read books by women if you're a man; to read books by people of your own ethnicity and also other ethnicities. Too many white readers read black authors only because it's Black History Month or for some other specific reason, yet black authors have written a disproportionate number of the best American books of the last century. We should all read poetry. We should read what makes us uncomfortable or challenges us. We should read not just the books we've been told will be good for our careers, not just the trendiest books, not just those written in the last thirty years. Read *Gulliver's Travels* and *The Iliad* and Wallace Stevens's poems. Read small-press books and literary magazines. And, of course, read the books into which you fall as into a warm bed on a cold night.

Don't read for technique—you'll pick that up without noticing it. Read to have your life changed. Read to develop a sense of shape and form—what makes works of art feel right, feel complete—and then, as you revise your own work, listen for the messages from within you that say, "No, no—a little more" or "Stop here" or "Slow down—*now* speed up!"

Where Should You Try to Publish?

Presumably you are reading some literary magazines. Subscribe to a few, and when someone has a reason to give you a present, ask for a subscription to another magazine you think you'd like, in print or online. Read at least something from any magazine to which you consider sending work. Then, when it comes time to submit, your taste will direct you. If you write flash fiction, you'll choose different magazines than if you're writing something long, quiet, and old-fashioned. Aim high but be realistic. The *New Yorker* publishes many more stories in a year than most literary quarterlies, and it's always looking for new writers. Read ten stories in the *New Yorker*, one after another, and then decide whether your stuff might be what interests them—don't assume it isn't. Try good literary quarterlies as well, and online magazines you like. Study Web sites to learn all you can about a magazine, including its submission procedures—each one is slightly different. Some insist on receiving submissions online; others want hard copy. Some allow submissions being considered elsewhere, and others don't. And so on.

When it comes to placing a book, consider competitions, small presses, and university presses, not just mainstream publishing houses. For much serious writing, small and university presses are the best solution. Their editors understand the books, are excited about them, want them, and know who wants to read them. This is true for almost all poetry, almost all collections of short stories and personal essays, and many memoirs, nonfiction books, and novels. I heard the author of a memoir describe her search for a publisher, which she conducted at an Association of Writers & Writing Programs (AWP) book fair. She walked up and down the aisles looking at books, and discovered a university press that seemed particularly open to memoirs with subject matter like hers; she talked to the people at the table (people at tables in book fairs want passersby to talk to them!) and eventually published with them. Not all books, of course, fall easily into categories. Certainly if your memoir or novel or book of essays or stories does fall into a category—if it's about, for example, religion, gay life, race, travel, mental health, farming, food, outdoor life—it makes sense to look for publishers who particularly welcome books like it. It may also be a good idea to look for a small or university press from a particular region if your book is set there.

For a novel or stories, if you too find yourself studying books at the AWP fair or in a good independent bookstore that offers both mainstream and small-press books, find and buy a few that look as if they may resemble yours. If a press publishes many books about young rock musicians or dystopian societies or vampires, you may not want to offer them your novel about a woman in her sixties reconsidering her faith. Note how much action and suspense there is in the books you carry home. If mainstream editors or agents have said your novel is good but they "just didn't fall in love with it," the problem is often that you don't have a sufficiently compelling story, and a small press may not care quite as much (or it may—make the story more compelling before you try).

On the other hand, if you've written a novel with a plot that has at least a little excitement, probably you'll try to find an agent who will place it with a mainstream press. Be prepared to try many agents, to rewrite your book twice more, to find publishing a job in its own right, with its own difficulties. But by all means, go for it. Through friends or Web sites, find agents who handle books of the sort you've written, and politely approach them. Their Web sites, again, will tell you just what to do—query first, e-mail a sample, whatever.

How Should You Submit Work?

Unless you've written a novel or a book-length memoir, don't send work out until you can submit several pieces at once, so you're not too caught up in the success of each one. Let them pile up a bit. Then, don't rush to send them everywhere at once. Some people send dozens of copies of the same story to different magazines—like finding customers for a pizza delivery business by leaving a flier on every doorknob in the city. Yet again, this is an occasion for common sense. It used to be that magazines didn't allow multiple submissions, and it was bad form to have to write to one and say, "I'd like to withdraw my story, which has been accepted elsewhere." Now most journals have no problem with multiple submissions—check the Web site. However, it stands to reason that if we all send out all our work to all of them all the time, there will not be enough people to read us. I regularly hear writers complain that the unpaid editors and interns at a magazine took a year or more to read a story—which the writer had sent to twenty places at once. Where's the sense in that? I don't say give up multiple submissions altogether, but if you respect your work and the editors whom you ask to read it, then you'll send a particular piece to particular magazines or editors for reasons—you won't just throw the stuff into the air and hope it lands on somebody receptive. Try a few magazines at once. If you try dozens, you're just overloading the system.

But the opposite reaction is worse. I mean, sending something to one place, checking the mailbox every day for a year, getting it back, taking to your bed, and sending it out again a year later. If you've decided to try for authorship—professional writing, writing for publication—then go about the task systematically, as you would if you were writing articles about socket wrenches for

Hardware Quarterly. Make lists of where you'd like to be published; devote some time to the clerical part of the job (when I was writing poems and had many wares to offer, I used to spend my writing hours every second Friday on it); keep several pieces of work out at once; maintain careful records, whether with some kind of software or just a list.

If you're submitting a book to agents, again, don't send a query to thirty agents in a morning. My own agent is now asking that initial inquiries come through the post office—doubtless because she was in danger of e-mail suffocation. Approach a particular agent for a reason, taking her or him seriously as a person. Agents need writers even more than writers need agents, and they have worked out ways to find you if in fact you're right for them. Respect their choices, and keep trying. It's important to remember that agents work with particular sorts of books and particular editors, and someone who says, "Your book has great merit but isn't right for me," may mean "I don't represent this sort of book," and the distinctions may be subtle. Sometimes if you write and say, "Can you suggest an agent who'll be more suitable?" you'll get a recommendation.

If forty agents all say it has great merit but they didn't fall in love, there is something wrong with the book—nine times out of ten, the writing is great but the story isn't compelling.

All this takes work, it's difficult—but it's not impossible. Magazines and publishing houses need writing to publish, and with persistence, hard work, and luck, you may be the author of the next piece they choose. It happens, often when you least expect it, and it's a good idea not to try too hard to figure it all out: just make a list of places you hope to publish in, and send everything, eventually, everywhere. When I was starting out, I'd often send two stories to a magazine at once, and when one was accepted, it was almost invariably not the one I had thought the magazine would prefer.

Be brave, be determined, and sooner or later it will work out. It's hard to publish, you may not publish as spectacularly as you hoped—but every writer I've known who has produced work I thought was good, who revised it (more times than anyone might expect), and who persisted in sending it out despite rejection, has eventually found editors who wanted to publish it.

What If It Doesn't Work?

You've tried again and again and again, done everything in this book and six other books, sent everything out to dozens of places, and nobody wants your stuff. Now what?

Most unpublished work I see is not hopeless but needs revising, even if it's been revised many times before. If you've really tried and tried and tried, and are willing to do *anything* to publish—and you've already been to writing school or have decided definitely not to go—be brave enough to think that there may be something large wrong.

If you're more wrecked by rejection than by the emotional experience of writing itself, or if you think of your task as getting control of the material, making it neat and orderly—rather than making it wild and *then* getting it under control—then possibly you're not really doing what writers have to do. Struggling writers have sometimes asked me what a story lacked that would make it publishable, and I've realized that they were imagining a series of rational, small fixes, when what they needed was emotional, and big. Sometimes, for example, a writer knows so well in advance what the point of the story will be, that she can't get out of its way;

all she can do is use the story to demonstrate what the characters are like and will always be like. Such writers can't detach themselves from the story enough to see it as a story rather than a statement of its theme. I can't easily explain what such people need to do, besides finding tangible actions to embody their characters' feelings. It has something to do with breaking down their own defenses, recognizing what they're doing, and writing the story again from the start, but with awareness of a reader.

If you're spending a lot of time and effort on publication and nothing is working and you really can't bring yourself to write that damned pile of stories yet again, then maybe you should write something else, something less emotionally demanding. Maybe it would be better to write opinion pieces, or reviews, or articles about topics of interest, like travel or social trends. If you inform yourself about other kinds of writing, you may learn how to write what somebody needs—you may even make some money. But whatever you do, as a self-respecting person, for heaven's sake *don't* just keep making yourself miserable. Maybe there *is* something that could be done with your fiction or memoir but you just can't grasp what it is. Well, that's not the same as being a serial killer. Forget it. There are other ways to spend your time.

Self-Publishing

Writing isn't really finished until someone reads what is written, as music requires ears and plays need an audience. Most of us, moreover, won't be able to do without publication by publishers: whatever part of the fantasy we're able to dispense with, we probably can't give up the approval of the stranger with a printing press—or a Web site—who chooses our work. I can't say much about self-publishing, never having tried it. If it would be satisfying for you, you've probably already made that decision and taken steps to make it happen. There haven't always been publishers standing between authors and printing presses; it isn't shameful to hire a printer.

But then—for me this would make self-publishing impossible— you have to do all the marketing yourself. You still need readers, still need the approval and pleasure of strangers, but you have no structure helping you get that, nothing like the message conveyed by a publisher's name: "Somebody besides the author thinks this is good." If you can market your own work relentlessly and cheerfully, good luck to you.

Once, decades ago, I gave a reading of my poems that turned out to be unsponsored. I was offered a place to do it, and only gradually realized I had to invite people, welcome them, provide refreshments, introduce myself, and then (gulp) read my poems. After the reading, which was fine, I said, "Never again do I bake my own brownies." I meant that I for one need somebody else to take on some of the responsibility, though I know I'll always have to do plenty of promotion myself (and part of my pleasure in publishing comes from the collaboration with editors, their assistants, and other people who work at the publishing house). As writers we each must figure out how we feel about baking our own brownies. Maybe you're fine with it. The rest of us need to find publishers— but we must stop assuming, both as readers and as writers, that the only respectable or authentic publication is mainstream press publication.

One possibility worth considering is a publishing collective or cooperative press. Perhaps you and other writers you know can start one: pool your energy and money on one of your books, and use the proceeds to publish the next, or try to secure grants from an arts council. My book of poems—my first book—was published by a cooperative press, Alice James Books, which still flourishes after forty years but no longer requires as much participation from authors (though authors who have published with the press still, as always, choose the new list). Poets whose books were accepted were not asked for money, but we did put in many hours of work. We weren't paid but were given many copies of our own books. I learned a great deal about the book business, made friends, and saw my book through the production process—an immensely satisfying experience. But I wasn't alone: there were other members of the cooperative to come up with ideas, fill orders, and teach me how to work on distribution and promotion.

The Part-Time Writer

There's a story we hear about how writers used to support themselves by writing full time that is partly true. Some decades ago, more magazines published fiction and paid well, and it was cheaper to live: writers of novels and short stories, maybe mixing in some journalism, maybe struggling, sometimes lived on their earnings. But the phrase "starving artist" and stories like the one in *La Bohème* tell us that, with few exceptions, creative people have long been poor. The poet Donald Hall has written about earning his living writing magazine articles, a textbook, and children's books to supplement what he could make from poetry: he gave up a tenured teaching job in the seventies and succeeded without it. Nowadays what he did probably wouldn't be possible, not without the consistent commercial success that is the fantasy we began this chapter with.

With few exceptions, every writer who isn't independently

wealthy does something else to earn a living and always has. It makes no sense to claim that people who write fiction along with another, more lucrative kind of writing (journalism, children's books) are writers, while fiction writers who teach in a university *aren't* writers. Or that *they're* writers, but people who write fiction while teaching fifth grade are not. Nor is it more authentic to wait tables or drive a taxi and write than to write while being a nurse or a computer programmer. A menial day job may make it easier for you to think—or it may make you so unaccustomed to expressing authority that you will be less able to take on authority on the page. A teacher, at least, will have learned to say, "You may do this but not that." So will a parent, and if you can stay home with kids and squeeze in a little writing time while a partner earns a living, good for you.

The real problem for the part-time writer is not how one is perceived but finding the time and emotional energy to write. One of my e-mail correspondents wrote me recently, wondering aloud, "Is it possible to write for twenty minutes at a time?" I would say no. I, at least, can't—or not unless I am so immersed in a project, it just rolls on the minute everything else pauses.

It seems to me that in order to write, she needs what I had back when I hired the babysitter and got serious about writing: two hours twice a week. Many writers can manage that—if they protect their time. Don't cheat children out of time (within reason!), but be wary of everyone else. Decide what your writing hours are, and learn to say no to people who want you to do other things during those hours. Be selfish, and take advantage of nice people who want to help.

Think of your need to write as a minor disability. It almost is, correct? You're a mess if you don't get it. If you had a worrisome symptom and a doctor said, "If you simply take two hours twice a week and nap, on a fixed schedule, you'll be fine," you'd find a way to do that. (My worrisome symptom is a bad temper.) Or think of your writing hours as something you've agreed to do in which other people's convenience is at stake. In an emergency you'd cancel a dentist's appointment—but otherwise you say to those who waylay you, "Sorry, I'm on my way to the dentist," and go. Name your computer, then say, "Sorry—I promised my friend Maxwell the whole afternoon."

Honor the work. It's a matter of believing—or pretending to believe, even when you don't—that you have the right to write, even if so far you haven't proved that the world needs your stories.

Once you have your time, however fiercely you've defended it, I'm afraid you need to do something else that may be difficult: squander it. Don't spend it doing anything but writing, don't leave the place where you write—but if necessary, just sit there, or read poetry. Give yourself time to think. If you make yourself sit still for two hours, you will probably come up with something to write, even if it's only a list of what's keeping you from knowing what the next scene of your story is. You'll have to make your own rules about what you're allowed to do while writing. I let myself check e-mail—it's too hard not to—but I don't write e-mails, except maybe a line to a good friend. I don't like browsing the Web (it's mostly irritating to someone with my eye defects); if you do, you'll need to establish limits and safeguards. You may need to put some kind of technological lock on it, making it temporarily unavailable. Cheating a bit and then suffering over that is fine—a small quantity of self-loathing is helpful to the process. But if you never get to the work during your two hours, figure out where to go or what to do that will keep you from distractions. Often leaving home helps. If the coffee shop has Wi-Fi, don't ask for the password.

Being Happy

Writing itself, once you get going, is a delightful pursuit—or so it seems to me—but much that surrounds writing, including the agonizing that often occurs before, during, after, and about publication, is unpleasant. The solution is to remember that we aren't just writers—we are persons of letters, as the late founder and director of the Bennington MFA program, Liam Rector, used to say. We are citizens of the republic of letters, and it turns out that being a citizen is the good part. Moreover, being an active citizen will make you feel powerful and protect you from turning into a literary Cinderella. Being a citizen of the republic of letters will make you happy. Writers have as much responsibility, after all, for helping good writing to thrive, as they do for writing their own dear books.

The wish to be a literary citizen—not to be alone with all this—is a large part of what draws people to MFA programs, I believe. Whether you join a writing community or not, there is still the available pleasure of discovering, buying, and reading obscure authors, and then telling others about them. You can do that one to one, or you can write reviews and essays about literature—it's harder than it used to be but still possible to find places that will print your reviews, or you can post them on Web sites or write a blog.

Citizens of the republic of letters can seek the pleasures of editing and teaching writing. The feeling of power you get from telling other people—in a helpful way!—what is wrong with their writing will help sustain you through the difficulties of your own soggy career. An organization in my town, at a big event a couple of times a year, pairs volunteers with high school students who need help writing college application essays; maybe your community has a similar program. Offer to be a preliminary reader for a magazine you like, and stop feeling like a victim. Start a magazine or even a small press—I know people who have done it—or volunteer to help with a magazine or press that already exists. Join with others to start a collective or cooperative press. Discover who in your area is doing letterpress publication; maybe take a class or raise money or otherwise offer to help.

Teach, if you think you'd enjoy helping other writers with their work. I know few activities more enjoyable, and someone always wants teaching. Teaching in a prison is immensely satisfying, as is running a writing group in a school, at a social club for people with mental illness, or in an old people's residence. When my youngest son was in first grade, I spent some weeks helping the first and second graders write stories: they had big sheets of paper with two lines for text and room to draw a picture. Writing is writing, and our discussions about it weren't too different from talking about writing with adults.

Formal, paid teaching of adults will help you feel like a citizen of the republic too, and if you have an MFA, you may be able to get work teaching writing in a community college, or part-time in a four-year college, even without many publications. Send your résumé to all the colleges in your area, and when a last-minute opening develops, they may call you. Full-time, tenure-track college teaching of writing requires substantial publications and often an MFA, sometimes a PhD, as well as a willingness to move to where the job is. For me, teaching in a low-residency MFA program has worked, though the pay is low and there are no benefits: we're at the college for only three weeks a year and otherwise work by correspondence from home.

Being a literary citizen can also mean getting involved in the connection between writers and the wider society: in PEN, in other organizations that work to benefit writers, in local arts councils, libraries, and schools. Doubtless there are many other possibilities for literary citizenship that I'm not thinking of. But do something; it will work better than almost anything else to make you feel you're really a writer.

One of my happiest experiences as a literary citizen, besides teaching, was editing a book about homelessness with two other women (neither of them writers). One woman interviewed people who were or had been homeless, while the second—who ran a small agency and had thought up the project—raised money, got people who worked with homeless clients to write about their jobs, and made everyone connected with the book, including the three of us, write answers to the questions What is home? What is neighborhood? and What is community? I line-edited: I pared everything down and turned it into grammatical English. The book, *As I Sat on the Green: Living Without a Home in New Haven*, was published by a homeless shelter.

Another good experience as a literary citizen was being one of four women who, for five years, ran the Ordinary Evening Reading Series: monthly readings of fiction, poetry, and occasional nonfiction in the basement of the great Anchor Bar in downtown New Haven. We invited authors we admired to come and read— apologetically, because we had no money to pay them—and everyone said yes; often, authors approached us to ask if we'd let them read. We took our readers out to dinner at an inexpensive restaurant (with our own money, because we couldn't be bothered to apply for grants or ask for contributions, though of course we should have), and we put people up in our houses if they came from out of town. Writers slept on my third floor, and I baked scones for breakfast. We had eighty-four distinguished writers over five years, and always had a good audience. People love hearing good writing in a bar, and if they've had a little to drink, they are more responsive. The bar liked it because we did it on Tuesdays—a slow night. We had famous people and people who are almost famous and people who should be famous. Again, the collaboration made it all a pleasure—planning, dealing with authors, writing publicity, giving introductions. We made it happen without even a mike or a podium: we used a music stand we called Matilda that we'd haul down to the basement of the bar; sometimes we forgot Matilda in restaurants and had to go back. I don't think anyone regretted reading in our series. Money all around would have been good, but doing it was what mattered—and in truth, though I believe in getting paid for one's labor, there was something inspiring about the writers' gift to us and our audience, our gift to them. We should all do what we can to be paid for our work and to pay others—but being paid is not the only value. Never assume a writer won't do what you want for the money you have available, or for nothing. Ask. Bake scones.

Above all, as a literary citizen, you need your own small city in the republic of writing—your friends. You need writing friends for more than praise or criticism; you need them for encouragement and to top your terrible stories. "Only two people came to your reading? That's nothing! *Nobody* came to mine!" You need friends who are writers because nobody else quite gets it. You need them to suggest books, to remember your work and talk about it months later, to assure you that the editor who just turned it down is a nitwit, to celebrate with you when you accomplish something you want. Sometimes you'll envy your friends, but envy is tolerable if you admit to yourself that you feel it. Let yourself think, "I want that too!" and you'll start to feel glad for your friend. Remind yourself that if you have friends who are getting classy rewards for their writing—praise, publication, prizes—then you are probably pretty classy yourself.

The business of writing is necessarily solitary. Most of us need to be alone to write. What we produce touches the solitude of someone else, the reader: with luck and work, we turn a private, ephemeral thought into something that enters a reader's consciousness, penetrating a different kind of privacy, starting up images. The images in the reader's mind may not be identical to those in the writer's. The writer pictures a round doorknob, but doesn't say so, and the reader's doorknob is oval, like one in her grandmother's house. But the reader has taken in what matters: the back door opens quickly; the man looking out sees one small red sneaker with white laces. He steps out into the sunshine, and writer and reader both squint. The reader takes in the human mystery, the tragedy and comedy. We work from solitude to solitude. It's a lonely business, and we need all the friends we can find.

The Writing Itself

We each should try to be as clearheaded, self-aware, and informed about writing as we are about buying a refrigerator. No, that's impossible—it's too emotional for that degree of clarity. But maybe we can be as clearheaded, self-aware, and informed about it as we are about adopting a dog or cat, negotiating a job, or staying healthy. Too many people are fairly sensible about those things but, first, tie their sense of worth as writers to greater success than is likely, and, second, fail to do what's necessary to get the success they could have: taking advantage of possibilities, believing the praise they get, sending work out when someone who should know has encouraged that, aiming high. Aim as high as you can, but know yourself and the situation.

When my oldest son started kindergarten, I got a part-time

teaching job, one class a term, and after that I combined writing, child care, and teaching, and thought of myself, again, as an English teacher—what I'd been before I had kids. One term, after several years of this routine, my class was canceled at the last minute. Though it paid so badly that the financial loss was minor, I was devastated—who *was* I, I reasoned, if I was not a teacher, if teaching could vanish with one regretful phone call? Then it occurred to me that maybe I was no longer primarily a teacher. Maybe I was a *writer*. I was writing poems that were mostly unpublished and stories that were all unpublished. I thought about this question for weeks, about what I didn't like about writing, and I noticed that it had eight disadvantages. That was many years ago, and I have discovered no others. The disadvantages are these: no money; no respect; no response for a long time to what you've written; no structure helping you to get started; no structure warding off interruptions ("I'm sorry, she's in a meeting"); no guarantee that you'll ever write anything that does anyone any good; no guarantee that, even if you do, the particular piece you're writing right now is worth your time; and no colleagues. I decided I would be a writer, despite the disadvantages—some of which, it turns out, diminish. Interruptions lessened when my kids got bigger, increased during their long and welcome vacations from college (some interruptions are worth it), diminished again when they began their adult lives. My parents became frail and interruptions increased. Now they've been dead for years, but now I have grandchildren. I love to spend time with them—mostly not during writing time. As for colleagues, I've found them through teaching, and I've learned to get started without a structure. I occasionally get money and respect. It works out.

The advantage of being a writer, after all, is big: the pleasure of it, the pleasure of words, the pleasure of *telling a story*. Lots of people dislike writing. You and I are the people who think it's a delight, at least sometimes. Our delight is what we get to keep, whatever happens, and I wish you many hours of it.

One last thing: be ambitious, in the best sense. Write—write first drafts—when you're sleepy and stupid, receptive and vulnerable. Make yourself safe from interruption for a time, whether by enforcing rules and schedules, by leaving home, or by playing music so loud that you can't hear anything outside the room—and then let come what may, however crazy and embarrassing and unformed and intense and unsettling the writing is. Your chance to be original and meaningful depends on the degree to which you can let out what is inside you that you don't quite know about and might prefer to keep on not knowing about. Take outrageous risks, and then have the patience and humility to fix your work. With a long, sturdy string tied to your kite, go out on the windiest day of the year, toss it into the sky, and see what happens.

Acknowledgments

Thanks to my students in the Bennington MFA program, to students and alumni who have become my friends though I never taught them, and to the writers I've met and taught elsewhere. Thank you for your wonderful minds and your willingness to think out loud. You inspire and teach me.

Thanks to my colleagues at Bennington, a bunch of geniuses from whom I learn all the time.

Thanks to Zoë Pagnamenta, my incomparable agent, who suggested that I write this book, and to Carole DeSanti and Christopher Russell, brilliant and kind editors. Thanks to Lynn Buckley, who created this book's jacket, and Nancy Resnick, who designed its interior.

My gratitude to those who read early drafts, made helpful suggestions, and encouraged me: April Bernard, Susan Hulsman Bingham, Donald Hall, Susan Holahan, Edward Mattison (who read several thousand interim and partial drafts), and Sandi Kahn Shelton.

Thanks to Craig Sklar, M.D., whose help keeps me seeing, and to William Padula, O.D., who for decades has prescribed lenses that enable me to read and write.

Chapter 8, "Silence and Storytelling" (based on a lecture delivered at Bennington College in January 2007), is dedicated to the memory of Liam Rector, the MFA program's founder and first director, and a passionate advocate for free speech all his life.

Thanks to Nina Mattison for the names Classico, Ungartino, Katchenary, and Yarley in Chapter 8, and to all my family for good talk, reasons to laugh, technical assistance, and general goodwill and sweetness.

The author of the useful phrase "sadistic ingenuity" is Stefani Nellen.

Appendix: Books Mentioned

Many of the stories, poems, and novels listed below are available in more than one edition. I've supplied names of publishers only when that's not the case.

Akhmatova, Anna. *The Word That Causes Death's Defeat: Poems of Memory.* Translated, with an introductory biography, critical essays, and commentary, by Nancy K. Anderson. New Haven: Yale University Press, 2004.

Austen, Jane. *Emma.* 1815.

Brontë, Charlotte. *Jane Eyre.* 1847.

———. *Villette.* 1853.

Carroll, Lewis. *Alice's Adventures in Wonderland.* 1865.

Cather, Willa. *The Song of the Lark.* 1915.

Cervantes, Miguel de. *Don Quixote.* 1615. Translated by Edith Grossman. New York: HarperCollins, 2003.

Costello, Mary. *Academy Street.* New York: Farrar, Straus and Giroux, 2015.

Dickens, Charles. *David Copperfield.* 1850.

———. *Great Expectations.* 1861.

Dubus, Andre. "The Winter Father." In *Selected Stories.* New York: Vintage Books, 1996.

Eliot, George. *The Journals of George Eliot.* Edited by Margaret Harris and Judith Johnston. Cambridge: Cambridge University Press, 1998.

————. *Middlemarch,* 1874.

————. *Quarry for Middlemarch.* Edited, with an introduction and notes, by Anna Theresa Kitchel. Berkeley: University of California Press [to accompany *Nineteenth Century Fiction,* Volume 4], 1950. For a facsimile of the quarry, see http://pds.lib.harvard.edu/pds/view/ 3552455 7.

Everyman. Fifteenth-century morality play.

Faulkner, William. *Absalom, Absalom!* 1936 (text corrected 1986).

Fitzgerald, F. Scott. *The Great Gatsby.* 1925.

Forster, E. M. *Aspects of the Novel.* 1927.

————. *Howards End.* 1910.

Gardner, John. *On Becoming a Novelist.* 1983.

Gissing, George. *The Odd Women.* 1893.

Heller, Zoë. *What Was She Thinking? [Notes on a Scandal].* New York: Picador, 2003.

Hemingway, Ernest. *The Sun Also Rises.* 1926.

Hill, Hamlin. *Mark Twain: God's Fool.* Chicago: University of Chicago Press, 1973.

James, Henry. *The Portrait of a Lady.* 1881.

James, P. D. *An Unsuitable Job for a Woman.* 1972. New York: Touchstone, 2001.

Jones, Edward P. "The Sunday Following Mother's Day." In *Lost in the City.* 1992.

Joyce, James. "A Painful Case." In *Dubliners.* 1914.

————. *A Portrait of the Artist as a Young Man.* 1916.

Lessing, Doris. *Alfred and Emily.* New York: Harper Perennial, 2008.

Mann, Thomas. *The Magic Mountain.* Translated by John E. Woods. New York: Everyman's Library, 2005.

Marshall, Paule. *Daughters.* New York: Atheneum, 1991.

Maxwell, William. *Ancestors.* 1971.

————. *The Chateau.* 1961.

————. *The Folded Leaf.* 1945.

————. *So Long, See You Tomorrow.* 1980.

————. *They Came Like Swallows.* 1937.

Melville, Herman. *Moby-Dick.* 1851.

Munro, Alice. "Cortes Island." In *The Love of a Good Woman*. 1998.

O'Connor, Flannery. "A Good Man Is Hard to Find." Story. 1953.

Olsen, Tillie. *Silences*. 1978.

———. *Tell Me a Riddle, Requa I, and Other Works*. With an introduction by Rebekah Edwards. Lincoln: University of Nebraska Press, 2013.

———. *Yonnondio: From the Thirties*. 1974.

Paley, Grace. "A Conversation with My Father." In *Enormous Changes at the Last Minute*. New York: Farrar, Straus and Giroux, 1974.

Powell, Dawn. *My Home Is Far Away*. 1944. South Royalton, VT: Steerforth Press, 1995.

Reid, Panthea. *Tillie Olsen. One Woman, Many Riddles*. New Brunswick, NJ: Rutgers University Press, 2010.

Roth, Henry. *Call It Sleep*. 1934.

Shakespeare, William. *King Lear*. 1605 or 1606.

———. *A Midsummer Night's Dream*. 1590s.

Spark, Muriel. *The Prime of Miss Jean Brodie*. 1961.

St. Aubyn, Edward. *The Patrick Melrose Novels: Never Mind, Bad News, Some Hope, Mother's Milk, At Last*. New York: Picador, 2012.

Stevens, Wallace. "Anecdote of the Jar." Poem. 1919.

Sturgis, Howard. *Belchamber*. 1904. New York: New York Review Books, 2008.

Swift, Jonathan. *Gulliver's Travels*. 1726.

Taylor, Elizabeth. *A Game of Hide and Seek*. 1951.

Twain, Mark. *The Mysterious Stranger Manuscripts*. Edited by William M. Gibson. Berkeley: University of California Press, 1969.

Welty, Eudora. *The Optimist's Daughter*. 1972.

West, Rebecca. *The Fountain Overflows*. 1956.

Woolf, Virginia. *A Room of One's Own*. 1929.

Yates, Richard. *Revolutionary Road*. 1961. New York: Vintage, 2000.

Index